WITHDRAWN
UTSA LIBRARIES

THE BLACK MAN'S PLACE IN SOUTH AFRICA

BY

PETER NIELSEN.

NEGRO UNIVERSITIES PRESS
WESTPORT, CONNECTICUT

Originally published in 1922
by Juta & Co., Ltd., Cape Town

Reprinted in 1970 by
Negro Universities Press
A Division of Greenwood Press, Inc.
Westport, Connecticut

Library of Congress Catalogue Card Number 70-109347

SBN 8371-3619-9

Printed in the United States of America

The University of Texas
At San Antonio

To

MY MOTHER.

PREFACE.

The reader has a right to ask what qualification the writer may have for dealing with the subject upon which he offers his opinions.

The author of this book claims the qualifications of an observer who, during many years, has studied the ways and thoughts of the Natives of South Africa on the spot, not through interpreters, but at first hand, through the medium of their own speech, which he professes to know as well as the Natives themselves.

P.N.

THE BLACK MAN'S PLACE IN SOUTH AFRICA.

THE QUESTION STATED.

The white man has taken up the burden of ruling his dark-skinned fellows throughout the world, and in South Africa he has so far carried that burden alone, feeling well assured of his fitness for the task. He has seen before him a feeble folk, strong only in their numbers and fit only for service, a people unworthy of sharing with his own race the privileges of social and political life, and it has seemed right therefore in his sight that this people should continue to bend under his dominant will. But to-day the white man is being disturbed by signs of coming strength among the black and thriving masses; signs of the awakening of a consciousness of racial manhood that is beginning to find voice in a demand for those rights of citizenship which hitherto have been so easily withheld. The white people are beginning to ask themselves whether they shall sit still and wait till that voice becomes clamant and insistent throughout the land or whether they shall begin now to think out and provide means for dealing with those coming events whose shadows are already falling athwart the immediate outlook. The strong and solid feeling among the whites in the past against giving any political rights to the blacks however civilised they might be is not so strong or as solid as it was. The number is growing of those among the ruling race who feel that the right of representation should here also follow the burden of taxation, but while there are many who think thus, those who try to think the matter out in all its bearings soon come to apprehend the possibility that where once political equality has been granted social equality may follow, and this apprehension makes the thinking man pause to think again before he commits himself to a definite and settled opinion.

Taking the civilisation of to-day to mean an ordered and advanced state of society in which all men are equally bound and entitled to share the burdens and privileges of the whole political and social life according to their individual limitations we ask whether the African Natives are capable of acquiring this civilisation, and whether, if it be proved that their capacity for progress is equal to that of the Europeans, the demand for full racial equality that must inevitably follow can in fairness be denied. This I take to be the crux of the Native Question in South Africa.

Before we attempt to answer this question it is necessary to find out, if we can, in what ways the African differs from the European ; for if it be found that there are radical and inherent differences between the two races of a kind that seem certain to remain unaltered by new influences and changed environment then the whites will feel justified in denying equality where nature herself has made it impossible, whereas if the existing difference be proved to be only outwardly acquired and not inwardly heritable then the coming demand for equality will stand supported by natural right which may not be ignored. The question, then, before us is this. Is the African Native equal to the European in mental and moral capacity or is he not ? We must have an answer to this question, for we cannot assign to the Native his proper place in the general scheme of our civilisation till we know exactly what manner of man he is.

We of to-day are rightly proud of our freedom from the sour superstitions and religious animosities of the past, but these hindrances to progress and general happiness were only dispelled by the light of scientific thought and clear reasoning. Let us then bring to bear that same blessed light upon our present enquiry into the reasons, real or fancied, for those prejudices of race and colour which we still retain, for it is only by removing the misconceptions and false notions that obscure our view that we can come to a clear understanding of the many complex issues that make up the great Native problem of Africa.

Bodily Differences.

"That which distinguishes man from the beast," said Beaumarchais, "is drinking without being thirsty, and making love at all seasons," and he spoke perhaps truer than he knew, for the fact that man is not bound by seasons and is not in entire subjection to his environment is the cardinal distinction between him and the brutes. This distinction was won through man's possession of a thinking brain which caused or coincided with an upright carriage whereby his two hands were set free from the lowly service of mere locomotion to make fire and to fashion the tools wherewith he was enabled to control his environment instead of remaining like the animals entirely controlled by it. This wonderful brain also made possible the communication and tradition of his experiences and ideas through articulate speech by which means his successors in each generation were able to keep and develop the slowly spelt lessons of human life.

Are the African Natives as far removed from the beasts as the Europeans, and do they share equally with the Europeans this great human distinction of ability to think?

The belief, at one time commonly held, that in morphological development and physical appearance the Bantu stand nearer in the scale of evolution to our common ape-like ancestors than do the white people does not seem to be warranted by facts.

Careful investigations by trained observers all over the world have shown that the various simian features discernible in the anatomy of modern man are found fairly evenly distributed amongst advanced and backward races.

The so-called prognathism of the Bantu has been cited as a racial mark denoting comparative nearness to the brutes, but when it is noted that anthropologists differ among themselves as to what constitutes this feature, whether it is to be measured from points above or below the nose or both, and when we are informed in some text books that while the negroes are prognathous, bushmen must be classed with Europeans as being the opposite, that is, orthognathous,[1] and when, added to this, we learn from other quarters that white women are, on the average, more prognathous than white men,[2] then the significance of this distinction, which in any case is not regarded as being relative to cranical capacity, is seen to be more apparent than real.

---

[1] Article on Anthropology in Nelson's Encyclopædia. The "gnathic index" is said to show that Europeans and Bushmen are orthognathous.

[2] "Man and Woman" by Havelock Ellis.

Extreme hairiness of body, on the other hand, which might well be taken as a simian or vestigial character, is seldom met with in the Bantu, but is equally common among Europeans and Australian aboriginals and is found particularly developed in the Ainu of Japan. The texture also of the African's hair is less like that of the hair of the man-like apes than is the hair of the European. The proportions of the limbs of the Europeans seem, on the average, to be nearer to the supposed prototype of man than those of the Bantu. The specifically human development of the red lips is more pronounced in the African than in the European,[3] and if there is anything in what has been called the " god-like erectness of the human carriage " then it must be admitted that the Bantu women exhibit a straightness of form which may well be envied by the ladies of civilisation.

It is generally accepted that the African Natives have a bodily odour of their own which is *sui generis* in that it is supposed to be different from that of other human races. Some early travellers have compared

---
[3] " The Mind of Primitive Man " by Franz Boas.

it with the smell of the female crocodile, and many people believe it to be a racial characteristic denoting a comparatively humble origin and intended by nature as a signal or warning for the rest of human kind against close physical contact with the African race. A recent student of the Negro question in America gives it as his opinion that this odour is "something which the Negroes will have difficulty in living down."[4] To most Europeans this smell seems to be more or less unpleasant but it must not be forgotten that it does not seem to affect the large numbers of white men of all nationalities who have found and still find pleasure in continued and intimate intercourse with African women. It would seem as if highly "refined" Europeans are nowadays given to exaggerate the sensation produced on their over delicate olfactory nerves by the exhalations caused by perspiration through a healthy and porous skin. In many of the so-called Ladies' Journals published in England and America advertisements appear regularly vaunting chemical preparations for the disguising of the odour of perspiration

---

[4] "Children of the Slaves" by Stephen Graham.

which, it is alleged, mars the attractiveness of women. If this is so it would seem that the nostrils of the modern European are rather too easily offended by the natural smell of his kind. However this may be there is no evidence for believing that the African's bodily smell is more animal-like than that of any other race.

If there is one thing which the white man of South Africa is sure about it is the comparative thickness of the "nigger skull," but this notion also would appear to be one of the many which have no foundation in fact.

The opinion of medical men, based upon actual observation and measurement, is to the effect that there is no evidence to support the contention that the Native skull is thicker than that of the European.[5] That the thick, woolly hair of the Native may account for his supposed comparative invulnerability to head injuries has not occurred to the layman observer who is more often

---

[5] "Anthropological Notes on Bantu Natives from Portuguese East Africa" by C. D. Maynard, F.R.C.S.E., Statistician and Clinician to the South African Institute for Medical Research, and G. A. Turner, M.B., B.Ch., Aberdeen D.P.H., Medical Officer to the Witwatersrand Native Labour Association.

given to vehement assertion than to careful enquiry.

The supposed arrest of the brain of the Bantu at the age of puberty owing to the closing of the sutures of the skull at an earlier age than happens with Europeans is another popular notion for which a sort of pseudo-scientific authority may be quoted from encyclopædias and old books of travel. The opinion of modern authorities on this subject is that those who say that the closure of the sutures of the skull determines brain growth would or should also say that the cart pulls the horse, for, if the sutures of the Native skull close at a somewhat earlier date in the average Native than in the average European then it simply means that the Native reaches maturity slightly earlier than the average white man.

The loss of mental alertness which is said by some to be peculiar to the Natives at the time of puberty is very often met with in the European youth or girl at that period of life. Competent observers have of late years come to the conclusion that this supposed falling off in intelligence, in so far as it may differ in degree from what has so often been noticed in European boys and girls at that point of development, is due to psychological and not to physiological causes. It is realised that this lapse in mental power of concentration in European youth in the stage of early adolescence is prevented by the force of example and fear of parental and general reprobation coupled with unbroken school-discipline, all of which factors are as yet seldom present in the surroundings of the average Bantu boy or girl.

The outward ethnic differentiæ of the Bantu are admittedly palpable and patent to everyone, but in the opinion of competent observers there is nothing in the anatomy of the black man to make him a lower beast than the man with the white skin. It is now seen that there is no apparent relation between complexion or skull shape and intelligence, but while this is so there appears to be a correlation between the size of the brain and the number of cells and fibres of which it is made up, although this correlation is so weak as to be difficult of demonstration.[6]

---

[6] "The Growth of the Brain" by H. H. Donaldson, Professor of Neurology in the University of Chicago.

The capacity of the normal human cranium varies from 1,000 cubic centimetres to 1,800 cubic centimetres, the mean capacity of female crania being 10 per cent. less than the mean of male crania. On this basis skulls are classified in the text books as being *microcephalic* when below 1,350 cubic centimetres, such as those of the extinct Tasmanians, Bushmen, Andamanese, Melanesians, Veddahs, and the Hill-men of India ; *mesocephalic*, those from 1,350 to 1,450 cubic centimetres, comprising Negroes, Malays, Amercian Indians, and Polynesians ; and *megacephalic*, above 1,450 cubic centimetres, including Eskimos, Europeans, Mongolians, Burmese and Japanese. The mean capacity among Europeans is fixed at 1,500 cubic centimetres, and the average weight of the brain at 1,300 grams.

These figures show that the skull capacity of the average European is larger than that of the average Negro, and as it seems plausible that the greater the central nervous system, the higher will be the faculty of the race, and the greater its aptitude for mental achievements, the conclusion that the European is superior in this respect seems on the face of it to be well grounded. There are, however, certain relevant facts which qualify this inference, and these must be briefly considered.

The anthropologist Manouvrier measured thirty-five skulls of eminent white men and found them to be of an average capacity of 1,665 cubic centimetres as compared to 1,560 cubic centimetres general average derived from 110 ordinary individuals. On the other hand he found that the cranial capacity of forty-five murderers was 1,580 cubic centimetres, also superior to the general average. Professor Franz Boas, in discussing this experiment, says that most of the brain weights constituting the general series are obtained in anatomical institutes, and the individuals who find their way there are poorly developed on account of malnutrition and of life under unfavourable circumstances, while the eminent men represent a much better nourished class. As poor nourishment reduces the weight and size of the whole body, it will also reduce the size and weight of the brain.[7] Dr. Arthur Keith when dealing with the so-called Piltdown skull in his book "The Antiquity of Man" says to

---

[7] "The Mind of Primitive Man" by Franz Boas.

the same effect that the size of brain is a very imperfect index of mental ability in that we know that certain elements enter into the formation of the brain which take no direct part in our mental activity, so that a person who has been blessed with a great robust body and strong, massive limbs requires a greater outfit of mere tracts and nerve cells for the purposes of mere animal administration than the smaller person with trunk and limbs of a moderate size.[8]

It seems fair, therefore, to assume that the brain-weights of big men of the Zulu, the Xosa and the Fingo tribes will be considerably above those of European women, but to conclude from this that the capacity of the big black man is higher than that of the average white woman would hardly be possible to-day. I would say here that I do not accept the suggestion, recently advanced, that the mental faculty of woman is qualitatively different from that of man. I hold that there is no difference of any kind between the intellectual powers of the male and female human being. The comparative lack

---

[8] "The Antiquity of Man" by Arthur Keith, M.D., LL.D., F.R.C.S., F.R.S.

of mental achievement on the part of women in the past I believe to have been due to a natural, and, as I think, wholesome feminine disinclination to take up intellectual studies and scientific pursuits that until recently have been deemed the prerogative of men, and not to any innate inferiority of the female brain.

According to Professor Sollas, whose high authority cannot be disputed, the size of the brain when looked at broadly seems to be connected with the taxinomic rank of the race, but when we come to details the connection between cranial capacity and mental endowment becomes less obvious. The Eskimo, for instance, who is of short stature, has a cranial capacity of 1,550 cubic centimetres, thus surpassing some of the most civilised peoples of Europe, and yet no one of this race has so far startled the world with any kind of mental achievement. "The result," says Professor Sollas, "of numerous investigations carried out during the last quarter of a century is to show that, within certain limits, no discoverable relation exists between the magnitude of the brain—or even its gross anatomy—and intellectual power," and he illustrates this statement by a list giving the cranial capacities and brain-weights of a number of famous men which shows that though Bismarck had a skull capacity of 1,965 cubic centimetres, Liebniz, who attained to the highest flights of genius, had a cranium measuring only 1,422 cubic centimetres.

Dealing more particularly with the assumed relation between highly specialised mental faculties and the anatomy of the brain, as apart from its mere size, the same author cites the case of Dr. Georg Sauerwein, who was master of forty or fifty languages, and whose brain after his death at the age of 74 in December, 1904, was dissected by Dr. L. Stieda with the idea that, since it is known that the motor centre for speech is situated in what is called Broca's area, some connection between great linguistic powers and the size or complication of the frontal lobe might be found in this highly specialised brain, but the examination revealed nothing that could be correlated with Sauerwein's exceptional gift.[9]

---

[9] "Ancient Hunters" by W. J. Sollas, D.De., LL.D., Professor of Geology and Palæontology in the University of Oxford.

Professor R. R. Marett in his handbook on Anthropology says, in discussing the subject of race, " You will see it stated that the size of the brain cavity will serve to mark off one race from another. This is extremely doubtful, to put it mildly. No doubt the average European shows some advantage in this respect as compared, say, with the Bushmen. But then you have to write off so much for their respective types of body, a bigger body going in general with a bigger head, that in the end you find yourself comparing mere abstractions. Again, the European may be the first to cry off on the ground that comparisons are odious ; for some specimens of Neanderthal man, in sheer size of brain cavity, are said to give points to any of our modern poets and politicians . . . Nor, if the brain itself be examined after death, and the form and number of its convolutions compared, is this criterion of hereditary brain-power any more satisfactory. It might be possible in this way to detect the difference between an idiot and a person of normal intelligence, but not the difference between a fool and a genius."[10]

---

[10] " Anthropology " by R. R. Marett.

In his book, "The Human Body," Dr. Keith, in dealing with racial characters, begs his readers to break away from the common habit of speaking and thinking of various races as high and low. "High and low," he says, "refers to civilisation; it does not refer to the human body."[11]

The foregoing authoritative opinions serve to show that the Bantu, as compared with other races, labour under no apparent physiological disabilities to hinder them in the process of mental development. Let us now consider in the light of modern psychology upon first-hand and reliable evidence the allegation of mental inferiority that is constantly brought against these people.

The Mind of the Native.

The white man has conquered the earth and all its dark-skinned people, and when he thinks of his continued success in the struggle for supremacy he feels that he has a right to be proud of himself and his race. He looks upon the black man as the fool of the human family who has failed in every way, whereas he, the lord of creation, has achieved the impossible, and this comparison which

---
[11] "The Antiquity of Man" by Arthur Keith, M.D.

is so favourable to himself naturally leads him to set up achievement as the sole test of ability. If asked why the African Native has never accomplished anything at all comparable with the feats of the European or the Asiatic the average white man will answer, without hesitation, that it is because the Native has always lacked the necessary capacity.

The average white man has a more or less vague notion that his own proud position at the top of human society is the result of the continuous and assiduous use of the brain by his forefathers in the struggle for existence under the rigorous conditions of a northern climate during thousands of generations by which constant exercise the mental faculty of his race grew and increased till it became, in course of time, a heritable intellectual endowment, whereas the Natives of Africa by failing always to make use of whatever brain power they might have been blessed with in the beginning have suffered a continuous loss of mental capacity.

The idea that the evolution of the human intellect is a perpetually progressive process by means of the constant use of the brain in the pursuits of increasing civilisation towards the eventual attainment of god-like perfection is one that appeals strongly to the popular fancy, and its corollary, that those who fail during long periods to make full use of their mental equipment in the ways of advancing civilisation must gradually lose a part, if not the whole, of their original talents, is commonly accepted as being warranted by the teaching of modern science.

But science, as a body, does not support the view that bodily characters and modifications acquired by an individual during his lifetime are transmissible to his offspring; in other words, science does not, as a body, accept the theory that the effects of use and disuse in the parent are inherited by his children. Modern science does not, indeed, definitely foreclose discussion of the subject, but what it says is that the empirical issue is doubtful with a considerable balance against the supposed inheritance of acquired characters.

Very recently evidence has, indeed, been adduced to prove that " Initiative in animal evolution comes by stimulation, excitation and response in new conditions, and is followed by repetition of these phenomena until they result in structural modifications, transmitted and directed by selection and the law of genetics." The student who tenders this evidence is Dr. Walter Kidd[12] who claims that his observations of the growth of the hair of the harness-horse prove that the prolonged friction caused by the harness produces heritable effects in the pattern of the hairy coat of this animal. It is admitted by this observer that such momentary and acute stimuli as are involved in the mutilation of the human body by boring holes in the ears, knocking out teeth, and by circumcision, which practices have been followed by so-called savages during long ages, seldom, if ever, lead to inherited characters, but he maintains that the effect of prolonged friction by the collar on the hair on the under side of the neck of the harness-horse has produced marks or patterns in the same place on certain young foals born by these horses.

These observations must, of course, be submitted to strict examination before science

---

[12] "Initiative in Evolution" by Walter Kidd, M.D., F.R.S.E.

will pronounce its opinion. Meanwhile I may be allowed to cite what Dr. Kidd calls an "undesigned experiment," which to my mind goes far to prove that the effects of prolonged friction on the human body during many generations is not heritable. The custom followed by many Bantu tribes of producing in their women an elongation of the genital parts by constant manipulation must have been practiced during very many generations, certainly much longer than the comparatively recent harnessing of horses in England, for we know how tenaciously primitive people cling to their old customs, generation after generation, for thousands of years, and yet no instance has ever been noticed by these people, who are very observant in these matters, of any sign of such an inherited characteristic in any of their female children.

The ordinary layman, though he may feel strongly interested in the problems of heredity and evolution, has seldom the leisure or the opportunity for the careful study of biological data, and he must therefore leave these to the specialists in scientific enquiry, but he is by no means precluded from using his own common-sense in drawing conclusions from the ordinary plain facts of life observable around him. It is when we come to consider this most important question in its bearing upon the mental side of the human being that the ordinary layman feels himself to be no less competent to form an opinion than the trained man of science.

Is it possible, then, we ask, for the parent whose intellect has been developed through training in his lifetime to transmit to his children any portion of this acquired increment of mental capacity, or, putting the question in more concrete terms, is it possible for a parent to transmit to his offspring any part of that power to increase the size and quality of the brain which may be assumed to have resulted in his own case from mental exercise? The question must not be misunderstood. We do not ask whether clever parents do as a rule have clever children; what we want to know is whether the successive sharpening of the wits of generations of people does, or does not, eventually result in establishing a real and cumulative asset of mental capacity.

Seeing that universal education has only come about within the latter part of the last century it must be clear that the vast majority of the present generation of educated Europeans are descended from people who never had any of that education which so many people nowadays regard as essential to the development and growth of the intellectual powers. But although education has only recently become, in various degrees, common to all white people, the light of learning has always been kept burning, however dimly at times, in certain places and circles, and it may, perhaps, be possible to find people to-day who are the descendants of those favoured few who have enjoyed, during many unbroken generations, the privilege of liberal education. Now let us assume that there are at present a small number of such people in the forefront of the intellectual activity of the day, and then let us ask ourselves whether these leaders of thought who can claim long lineal descent from learned ancestors show any mental capacity over and above that which is displayed by those commoners who are also in the foremost ranks of thought and science, but who cannot lay claim to such continuous ancestral training.

If we admit the existence of two such separate classes to-day then the answer must surely be that there is no mental difference discernible between them. But I think we may safely conclude that there has been very little of the kind of descent here presumed. It would be well-nigh impossible to find people who could prove an unbroken lineage of educated forbears going back more than four hundred years. During the middle ages the monks of the Church were the chief and almost sole depositories of education and learning, and as they were bound by their vows to life-long celibacy there could be no transmission from them to posterity of any of that increased capacity of brain which we are supposing as having been acquired by each individual through his own mental exertion. We know, of course, that there were frequent lapses from the unnatural restraint imposed on these men so that some of them may have propagated their kind, but such illegitimate offspring was not likely to remain within the circle of learning and therefore could not perpetuate the line. We of to-day know full well that the son of the common labourer whose forefathers had no education can, with equality of opportunity, achieve as much and travel as far in any field of mental activity as can the scion of the oldest of our most favoured families.

There does not seem to have been any augmentation of human brain power since written records of events were begun. Indeed it would seem rather as if there had been in many places a decrease in intellectual capacity, as when we compare the fellahin of modern Egypt with their great ancestors whom they resemble so closely in physical appearance that there can be little doubt about the purity of their descent. The same may be said about the modern descendants of the people who created " the glory that was Greece and the grandeur that was Rome." And when we consider the period of the Renaissance we cannot say that civilised man of to-day is superior to those people who after centuries of stagnation and general illiteracy were yet able to seize and develop the long-forgotten wisdom and philosophy of antiquity.

To go still further back and to venture beyond the historical horizon into the dim past when prehistoric man roamed over

Europe is a task manifestly beyond the powers of the ordinary layman, and here we must, perforce, trust ourselves to the guidance of those students whose training and special learning entitle them to speak with authority.

The so-called Piltdown skull which was discovered in 1912 is accepted as representing the most ancient of human remains yet found in England, its age being estimated at somewhere between 250,000 and 500,000 years. In discussing the size and arrangement of the lobes and convolutions of the brain which this cranium must have contained, Dr. Arthur Keith, who is admittedly the highest authority on the subject to-day, makes the following statement: " Unfortunately our knowledge of the brain, greatly as it has increased of late years, has not yet reached the point at which we can say after close examination of all the features of a brain that its owner has reached this or that status. The statement which Huxley made about the ancient human skull from the cave of Engis still holds good of the brain : 'It might have belonged to a philosopher or might have contained the thoughtless mind of a savage.' That is only one side of our problem, there is another. Huxley's statement refers to the average brain, which is equal to the needs of both the philosopher and the savage. It does not in any way invalidate the truth that a small brain with a simple pattern of convolutions is a less capable organ than the large brain with a complex pattern. If then we find a fairly large brain in the Piltdown man, with an arrangement and development of convolutions not very unlike those of a modern man, we shall be justified in drawing the conclusion that, so far as potential mental ability is concerned, he has reached the modern standard. We must always keep in mind that accomplishments and inventions which seem so simple to us were new and unsolved problems to the pioneers who worked their way up from a simian to a human estate."

In his concluding remarks upon this important find, Dr. Keith iterates his opinion: " Although our knowledge of the human brain is limited—there are large areas to which we can assign no definite function—we may rest assured that a brain which was shaped in a mould so similar to our own was one which responded to the outside world as ours does. Piltdown man saw, heard, felt, thought and dreamt much as we still do. If the eoliths found in the same bed of gravel were his handiwork, then we can also say he had made a great stride towards that state which has culminated in the inventive civilisation of the modern western world."[13]

Professor Herbert Donaldson of the University of Chicago, gives it as his opinion that "In comparing remote times with the present, or in our own age, races which have reached distinction with those which have remained obscure, it is by no means clear that the grade of civilisation attained is associated with a corresponding enlargement in the nervous system, or with an increase in the mental capabilities of the best representatives of those communities."[14]

Now while the ordinary man is unable to pronounce judgment upon expert opinion he is quite capable of understanding the main arguments upon which the foregoing conclu-

---
[13] "The Antiquity of Man" by Arthur Keith, M.D.
[14] "The Growth of the Brain" by H. H. Donaldson.

sions are based. We all realise the truth of the old saying "Il n'y a que le premier pas qui coûte." We all appreciate the tremendous difficulty of taking the first step in the way of discovery and invention. We know that to be the first to step forward in an utterly new direction or venture ; to be the first to work out, without any guidance or previous education, the first principles, however simple, in the doing, or thinking out of anything new, requires a mental audacity and astuteness that predicate a brain capacity as great as that which enables modern man to apply and develop the accumulated knowledge available in the textbooks of to-day. Dr. Alfred Russell Wallace held strongly to this opinion. He could see no proof of continuously increasing intellectual power ; he thought that where the greatest advance in intellect is supposed to have been made this might be wholly due to the cumulative effect of successive acquisitions of knowledge handed down from age to age by written or printed books ; that Euclid and Archimedes were probably the equals of any of our greatest mathematicians of to-day ; and that we are entitled to believe that the higher intellectual and moral nature of man has been approximately stationary during the whole period of human history. This great and intrepid thinker states his view with characteristic incisiveness thus : " Many writers thoughtlessly speak of the hereditary effects of strength or skill due to any mechanical work or special art being continued generation after generation in the same family, as amongst the castes of India. But of any progressive improvement there is no evidence whatever. Those children who had a natural aptitude for the work would, of course, form the successors of their parents, and there is no proof of anything hereditary except as regards this innate aptitude. Many people are alarmed at the statement that the effects of education and training are not hereditary, and think that if that were really the case there would be no hope for improvement of the race ; but close consideration will show them that if the results of our education in the widest sense, in the home, in the shop, in the nation, and in the world at large, had really been hereditary, even in the slightest degree, then indeed there would be little hope for humanity, and there is no clearer proof of this than the fact that we have not *all* been made much worse—the wonder being that any fragment of morality, or humanity, or the love of truth or justice for their own sakes still exists among us."[15]

I think the majority of thoughtful people will agree that these words express their own observations. Every day we see how children have to be taught to act and behave. We see continually how parents have to put pressure on their children to make them accept and apply those moral principles and mental valuations which have guided their lives and the lives of thousands of generations before them. We know only too well that children do not inherit the moral standards of right and wrong of their parents, and that to establish these principles in the young is a matter of protracted and often painful inculcation. The proved maxim that honesty is the best policy is still being literally hammered into the children of to-day who seem to find it no easier to follow the better

---

[15] " Social Environment and Moral Progress " by Alfred Russell Wallace, O.M., D.C.L., Oxon.

way than did the children of the past. If mental modifications acquired by the parents were in any degree transmissible to the offspring then there would be no need for this constant repetition of the same process in every new generation.

The earliest indubitable man hitherto discovered was fully evolved when first met with, he was *homo sapiens*. By means of his human intelligence this frail, unspecialized being became in a sense the very lord of creation, for instead of remaining, like the animals, entirely subject to his surroundings he subjected his surroundings to himself. By means of this intelligence man was enabled to break away from the absolute rule of the law of natural selection which punishes with extinction all those types that fail in fitness for survival in the struggle for existence, so that, unlike the animals that die out when their particular structure does not fit in with their environment, man by means of his thinking brain was able to equip himself with parts of his environment, and thus to become its master. The process of evolution ceased to affect directly this creature who had a brain that could think, and ever since that brain was given to him man has remained unmoved and stationary above and apart from all other living things. All this is implied in the command, "Be ye fruitful and multiply and replenish the earth and subdue it."

But though man became almost emancipated from the direct servitude of natural selection, he still is, and always will be, subject to the law of heredity. Man is made up of a group of innate characters inherited from a very mixed ancestry, these characters, being innate, are transmissible to his offspring, but such characters as are acquired by the parent through the direct influence of education or other environment, not being innate are not transmissible to his children. But in so far as a new development of latent and innate characters, through the influence of the environment, may help or hinder certain types in propagating themselves, the race may, perhaps, be modified through such influence by the process of gradual elimination of the types that lack the characters that prove to be of survival value in a particular locality. This we may suppose might happen where a number of Europeans, composed half of blondes and half of brunettes, come to live in a tropical country, if it be proved that the comparative darkness of the brunettes afford them better protection against inimical light and heat than the fair skin of the blondes, so that the former would on the average, enjoy better health and live longer, and therefore have more children than the latter, whereby, in course of time, the appearance of these people would be modified in respect of the general complexion of their skin. This, it is easy to see, would not mean the acquisition of a new and heritable means of protection, but only a development in each individual of an already present innate character that happened to be well fitted for survival in a certain climatic zone.

In order, therefore, to obtain any direct modification of the race in the way of mental improvement the physical effect of education must be such as to ensure longer life and with it, the concomitant chance of greater fertility for those who are educated against those who are not, so that the latter would tend to die out while the former would continue to increase their numbers. In other words, education must prove to be of survival value. Seeing that where education has increased most the birth-rate has tended to decrease it seems clear that we cannot regard continuous mental training as a favourable factor in the competition of propagation of human varieties.

If then we accept the conclusion that the effects of individual experience are not cumulatively hereditary we shall cease to cavil at the fact that there has been no anatomical or structural progress in the human body or brain since the time when men first became social and civilised beings, that is to say, since they first began to work together with their heads and hands, and we shall see that that which was to be expected has always happened, in that, from the earliest historical times to the present day, human life has been as the rolling and unrolling of a carpet. Cycles of civilisations, all essentially similar, have been evolved, one after another, to endure for a while and then to fade away, leaving the raw material of human kind as it was from the beginning. There is no evidence of any advancement in physique, intellect or moral character. The leaders of mankind were the law-givers, whether they were witch doctors, priests, chiefs, prophets or kings, and they all sought to establish their laws by claiming supernatural delegation and authority. With writing came the codes, and when we compare the statutes of Hammurabi, who flourished about 2,200 years B.C., with those compiled by his successors, Moses, Solon, Justinian and Napoleon, we find in them all evidence of the same mental appreciation and capacity in dealing with the social conditions and problems of their respective periods. The greatest products of art are still met with in the sculptured forms of ancient Greece, those images of serene beauty which may be imitated but not excelled. The reasoning powers of the ancient philosophers who, long before Christ was born, debated the still unanswered riddles of existence, when we compare the paucity of data on which they had to work with the wealth of knowledge now available, must be ranked as high as the intellectual ability of our foremost thinkers of to-day. In mechanical proficiency the world has indeed advanced to an astonishing extent, but the perfection of our modern machinery means only a gradual and very recent advance upon earlier methods and does not denote a corresponding development in the mind itself. The Greeks had no machinery to speak of, neither had the English in the days of Shakespeare and Newton, but who can doubt that the engineers of those times would have been equal to the task of understanding and applying the principles of modern mechanics had the necessary books been available to them? We do not assume that because the modern Germans excel as chemists they are therefore blessed with higher reasoning ability than were the contemporaries of Socrates and Plato who had no knowledge of the science of chemistry. The conclusion forced upon us after a sober and impartial survey of the facts of history is that, although the intellectual output of the world is always increasing, the intellect itself remains unaltered. Knowledge, we see, is after all, only descriptive, never fundamental. We can describe the appearance and condition of a process, but not the way of it, and though knowledge has come in rich abundance, wisdom still lingers.

The foregoing argument shows that the alleged mental superiority of the European cannot be due to constant use or education, so that it now becomes necessary for those who maintain that it nevertheless exists to prove, not only that the white man's intellectual capacity is now superior but to prove also that from the beginning it has always been stronger and better than that of the African Native, or, in other words, those who believe that the white race has inherent mental superiority must prove innate inferiority in the mental make-up of the Native.

There is a more or less indefinite notion abroad that the Bantu languages, as compared with those of Europe, are but poor and ineffective vehicles for the conveyance of abstract ideas, wherefore the capacity to form and entertain such ideas may be taken to be innately inferior in the Native brain. That the language of a people embodies, so to speak, in objective form the intellectual progress made by it is certainly true, and it will be well, therefore, to state briefly the actual and potential value of the Native speech as compared with that of the whites.

The living and the dead languages of the world have been classified by philologists into three main types of linguistic morphology; the isolating, like Chinese; the agglutinative, like Turkish and Bantu, and the inflective, like Latin. It was customary not long ago to look upon these three types as steps in a process of historical development, the isolating representing the most primitive form of speech at which it was possible to arrive, the agglutinative coming next in order as a type evolved from the isolating, and the inflective as the latest and so-called highest type of all. But since the matter has been carefully studied it has been admitted that there is no satisfactory evidence for believing in any evolution of linguistic types. English is now considered to be an isolating language in the making while Chinese is cited by authoritative European scholars as being a language which with the simplest possible means at its disposal can express the most technical or philosophical ideas with absolute freedom from ambiguity and with admirable conciseness and direction.[16]

---

[16] "The Varieties of Human Speech" by Edward Sapier, in Smithsonian Institute Report for 1912.

While I do not pretend to philological authority I do claim the ability to make a sound comparison between the main Bantu languages which I know and those European languages with which I happen to be familiar, and I have no hesitation in saying that though the Bantu types are not at present as fully developed in point of simplicity and preciseness as are the main languages of Europe they are, nevertheless, by reason of their peculiar genius, capable of being rapidly developed into as perfect a means for the expression of human thought as any of the European types of speech; they are astonishingly rich in verbs which make it easy to express motion and action clearly and vividly; the impersonal, or abstract article "it" is used exactly as in European languages, and the particular prefix provided in some of the Bantu types for the class of nouns which represent abstract conceptions makes it possible to increase the vocabularies in that direction *ad infinitum.* The Bantu types are not so-called holophrastic forms of primitive speech in which the compounding of expressions is said to take the place of the conveyance of ideas, nor are they made up of onomatopoetic, or interjectional expressions, if indeed such languages exist anywhere outside the heads of the half-informed. They are languages equal in potential capacity to any included in the main Indo-European group. Even now in their comparatively undeveloped state these languages are capable of expressing the subtleties of early philosophical speculation. I would not, for instance, feel daunted if I were set the task of translating into any of these main types, say, the dialectics of Socrates. To do this I would first reduce the more complex terms to such simple and common Anglo-Saxon words as when built together would give the same meaning, and then translate these into their Bantu equivalents. The substitution of Anglo-Saxon words for those of modern English would, no doubt, involve a good deal of repetition but the sense would be adequately rendered. I would proceed in the same way as the early teachers and writers who had to build up the language they used as they went along. The English indeed, have not built up their world-wide speech with their own materials but have, with characteristic acquisitiveness taken the combinations they wanted, ready made, mainly from Greek, Latin and French. How far and how well a Native would understand my presentation of metaphysical speculation would depend upon the degree of familiarity he might have acquired, through Missionary teaching or otherwise, with abstract notions in general. In my opinion the average "raw" Native would understand as well and as much as the average uneducated European peasant. Both would probably find my disquisition "sad stuff"; both would require time for that repetition of the words which is necessary to familiarise the mind with the unaccustomed ideas they represent; in both cases one would have to "give them the words that the ideas may come." A single illustration will show my meaning. When the first Missionaries rendered the word "soul" into Zulu by the word signifying "breath" in that language they simply followed the example of their predecessors of antiquity who employed the Latin *spiritus*, which also means "breath," for the same purpose, namely, to convey to their hearers the idea of a breath-like or ethereal something housed in, but separable from, the human body.

" The essence of language," said Aristotle, " is that it should be clear and not mean." The raw Bantu material is ample for compliance with this demand, and the process of development will not be as protracted as in early Europe for it may be accomplished here, largely, by the simple means of translating the words already thought out and provided in the white man's language. In so far, then, as we attempt to measure the mentality of the Natives by their language we find that they cannot be relegated to a lower plane than that occupied by the uneducated peasantry of Europe of a few decades ago.

Most people are prepared to believe that the primary psychical processes are identical in all races, but many still profess to see a difference in favour of the white man in what they call the higher faculties of the mind. But the much-abused word " faculty " no longer bears the meaning given to it by Locke and his followers who propounded a limitless brood or set of faculties to correspond with every process discoverable by introspection as taking place in the mind. In modern psychology the word means simply a capacity for an ultimate, irreducible, or unanalysable mode of thinking of, or being conscious of, objects. Perception, for instance, is looked upon as the capacity for thinking of a thing immediately at hand, and memory as a capacity for thinking again of a certain material or abstract object. The mental power of abstraction is no longer considered as a sort of separate function of the mind but is regarded as the capacity for thinking of, say, whiteness as apart from any particular white patch. But the notion that the white man is endowed with a set of finer feelings and with special and higher powers of abstraction than is the African Native is so generally entertained that it will be convenient to make the necessary comparisons in, more or less, the commonly accepted terms.

Those who look upon the Native as being in every way a more primitive being than the European will naturally be disposed to believe that he is more a creature of instincts than a man of reason, and they will expect him to move in dependence upon certain fundamental intuitions where the

European goes guided by reason alone. I have found no evidence whatever to support this supposition.

The elementry instinct of self-preservation is no stronger in the Native than in the white man. Suicide is not at all uncommon among the Bantu. I. have seen many instances of Natives who have shown a calm and philosophical disregard of death where life has seemed no longer desirable. This pre-eminently human prerogative—for no animal can rise to the conscious and deliberate destruction of itself—has often been exercised, as I have seen, by Natives in their sound and sober senses so as to preclude entirely that suggestion of temporary insanity which is so commonly accepted at coroner's inquests in England and elsewhere.

The instinct of direction, the " bump of locality " as it is generally called, varies with the Natives as it does among the whites, and is no keener in the individual Native than in the individual white man. All the hunters and travellers I have met have confirmed the opinion I have myself formed from personal experience that by training his ordinary powers of observation and thereby developing his sense of locality and direction the average European is able, after a comparatively short time, to find his way in difficult country as well as the Natives, while some European hunters who have dispensed with Native guides and trackers have acquired the art of tracking game so well that they surpass even the local Natives themselves. "Veldcraft" is simply a matter of training the ordinary faculties of observation and memory for particular purposes, and the Native shows no such superiority in this respect as would naturally be expected from him if he were indeed better provided with animal instincts than the more civilised white man.

The sexual instincts of the Natives seem in no wise different from those of other people. The African male, like the European male, is generally more amative than the female who is always more philoprogenitive than the man. But the notion is common that the Native male is more bestial when sexually excited than the white man in similar case, and this is taken to account for the fact that he is so often found guilty of crimes of violence against females of his own colour, and sometimes even against European women.

It must be borne in mind that before the white man came the Natives, like the peasants in many European countries not long ago, conducted their courtship and love-making with a show of violence which seemed to them right and proper. The idea, indeed, that any self-respecting Native girl could yield herself to a lover without, at least, a semblance of physical resistance, leading to her more or less forcible capture by the man, would have seemed, and still seems, distinctly improper to the majority of Native women in their raw state. But since the European code was set up Native women have not been slow in making use of its protection, and, as I have seen, have not infrequently abused that protection by alleging rape or assault where their own action in simulating flight and resistance served, as they well knew it would, to stimulate passion and pursuit.

In considering crimes of violence against white women it must also be remembered that the Native "house-boy" who works in constant and close physical contact with his European mistress and her daughters is exposed to sexual excitation which very few European youths are called upon to withstand. But crimes of this kind are indeed common enough among the lower orders in Europe and America, and are particularly frequent among men who have to live for a long time in unnatural abstinence from natural intercourse with the opposite sex, and who then find themselves in new surroundings giving opportunities for the gratification of their natural desires, but without having at the same time the restraining influences of their home life to help them to overcome the temptations to which they are exposed. The seaports of Europe and America, and the Great War furnish too many sad examples of sexual ferocity by white men to allow us to think that they are in this respect inherently superior to the men of other races.

The maternal instinct is manifested in the same manner and degree in the women of both people. I have often asked Native women whether it would be possible for any mother among them to distinguish her own new-born baby from a supposed "changeling" of the same sex and of the same general appearance, and the answer has always been negative. The Native and the white woman alike would continue to cherish the substituted child exactly as they would have cherished the issue of their own bodies. The desire to bear children is the same in all normally constituted women irrespective of colour or race, and there is no sign of any special instinct for identification in the Native woman, such as the sense of smell, which is found in all the higher animals.

There are some students who think that most of the emotions of man are but the survivals of instinctive habit. Be this as it may, the sexual attraction which is commonly called love certainly seems to be essentially instinctive whereas friendship and parental and filial devotion, when continued throughout life, seem to be emotions that depend largely upon association and conscious intelligence. Every natural mother will sacrifice herself for her offspring while it is young but the tender feeling which continues in her breast towards the child after it has grown up is sustained by association, or, where the child is continually absent, by conscious intelligence in the form of considerations of conventional approbation which in time merge into a habit or a sense of duty which is hardly recognised as such. Many white people think that although the average Native mother is capable of the greatest devotion for her young children she is incapable of the love which a white mother feels for her children even after they have ceased to depend upon her care. This, I think, is wrong. I have seen many instances of elderly Native women who have cherished their grown up children to the last with every sign of motherly affection.

Joy and sorrow, love and hatred, hope and fear, these are the fundamental emotions of human kind. Can any difference be detected between these feelings in the two races?

No one who knows him will say that the Native's capacity for the "joy of life unquestioned" is less than that of the average white man. Most Natives are born lovers of song and music, and attain easily to technical proficiency in the art of harmony. The æsthetic sense is present in the average Native as it is in the average European and in both is easily overlooked when not stimulated and developed by education and culture. That the Natives, as a whole, feel the sorrows of life and death as keenly as do the people of other races will be readily admitted by all who know them well, although their way of showing their sorrow may differ from those prescribed by the canons of conduct of other communities.

It is assumed by many that love, "the grand passion," has been brought to a finer point, as it were, among the white people than anywhere else, and it may well be that monogamy is conducive to the growth of a higher and purer form of sexual reciprocity than is possible under the polygamous system of the Natives and other peoples. The monogamous marriage, though based on sexual attraction in the first instance, tends to become, as the man and the woman grow older, a union of souls, so to speak, more or less independent of the sexual element itself. The close and continued association of one man and one woman of compatible temperaments no doubt brings about a state of mutual intimacy, dependence and devotion which can hardly be possible in a polygamous household. But on the other hand may fairly be cited the frequent instances, familiar to all, of widows and widowers among

Europeans who, despite their repeated and quite honest protestations of undying and undivided love for the first " one and only " mate, nevertheless find speedy consolation in a second marriage in which undying and whole-hearted love for the second " one and only " spouse is again declared and accepted in all sincerity. The phenomenon of " falling in love," as it is commonly called, is not peculiar to white people. I have known many cases where the love-sick Native swain has travelled hundreds of miles and suffered great hardships in order to reach or recover the one woman of his choice though other women, no less desirable, were ready to be had for the asking at his home. The converse is even more commonly seen. Native women are remarkably like white women. They look upon marriage as their proper and natural function in life, but they are not all of them willing to marry according to parental instructions ; there is the same proportion of self-willed damsels among them as among the whites, who by obdurately refusing to enter into the marriages arranged for them cause pain and trouble to their well-meaning parents.

Jealousy, especially from the female side, is an ever-present source of trouble and unhappiness among the Natives. The length to which a jealous Native wife will go in winning back the affections of an errant husband is often extraordinary, though the ways and means she adopts differ but little from those practised by the superstitious and credulous peasantry in Europe less than a hundred years ago.

While no one will deny the African Native a capacity for feeling anger equal to that of the white man when provoked by insult and injury there are many who believe that he is constitutionally incapable of sustaining that feeling of hatred which in the European so often leads to premeditated and prepared revenge. This notion is, no doubt, derivable from the fact that a Native seldom shows any open vindictiveness against a European employer by whom he has been insulted or unjustly punished, but this fact may, I think, be otherwise accounted for. The white man's prestige, backed up as it is by the established powers of law and order, makes the attempt at revenge by a Native a difficult and risky undertaking and, furthermore, there is to be considered the spirit of traditional submissiveness which at all times and in all places marks the attitude of the slave or serf towards his master. One has only to remember the many accounts of abject resignation by the peasants of France and the moujiks of Russia before the revolutions that changed the order of the past in those countries. No such considerations affect the Native where his anger and hatred are directed against one or more of his own colour. The records of the South African courts are replete with instances of cattle-maiming, arson, poisoning and other crimes proved to have been motived solely by feelings of revenge.

Courage and fear are feelings that depend upon conditions that seem to be fairly evenly distributed all over the world, and where the virtue of courage in the form of pugnacity is comparatively lacking, as amongst the bulk of the population of India, other forms thereof are met with, such as that wonderful contempt of a painful death by burning which was so often displayed by the widows of that country in following their ancient custom of *suttee*. The average white man feels assured that no race can be compared in bravery with his own, and that within that race no nation can be found equal in courage to the one to which he belongs. This is a form of elemental patriotism common to all communities, but those who have shared the dangers of flood and field with African Natives often testify to acts of sublime courage by Native soldiers, hunters and miners in the face of real and appreciated danger under circumstances which show that the Natives as a whole are no less capable than the white people of conquering instinctive fear and of sacrificing the individual self when great demands are made. I am not speaking now of what is commonly called mob-courage. Natives have been known to go through fire and water alone as well as white men.

Is there any difference of kind or degree in the moral sense of the two races? In the prevailing view of authoritative students morality is emotional and not intellectual in its origin, and the warrant of right doing is attributed not to some hypothetical objective standard, but to the whisperings of an inner conscience, an innate subjective mental state, independent of environment and education. Differences, undoubtedly, exist as to the acts or omissions which are approved or disapproved by the moral feeling in the two races respectively, but the feeling is the same. The feelings which prompt a Native woman to condemn barrenness in other women is the same as that which makes the average European lady look upon immodesty as a sign of immorality. The difference is objective, not subjective; it is in the outlook but not in the inner sense. That immorality is rife amongst Natives no one who knows them well will deny, but neither can putanism amongst the whites be denied. Before the white man came the very robust moral sense of the Natives made them put down theft and, sometimes, adultery, with a thoroughness which is apparently impossible amongst the most civilised white people to-day. Now that Western civilisation is spreading over the lard the difference in the moral outlook of the two peoples tends to decrease; with the savage vices go the savage virtues, and soon there will be no difference at all.

Having found no difference between the senses, instincts and inner feelings of the two races we come now to consider the oft-alleged difference in what is popularly called *pure intellect* in favour of the white man. Is there such a thing as pure intellect or pure rationality? Obviously there is not. The thought that we call abstract is fashioned in the same way as the thought that is formed by the recognition of similarities between concrete objects. The abstract thought has its source like all other forms of thought in the organic and emotional structure of the individual, and it is, indeed, only by pointing to instances that we can define what we mean by an abstract idea. But many people still think that the white race is gifted with a special faculty for thinking about general attributes as apart from the particular objects in which the abstracted attributes may be concretely perceived. There is no foundation in fact for this presumption. The Natives have no difficulty in finding words wherewith to abstract the general essence from a plurality of facts or instances; their vocabulary is as apt and as extensive for this purpose as that which suffices for the mental or spiritual needs of the bulk of European people, indeed, the capacity for abstracting the general nature and character from the particular experience or emotion into pithy expressions by way of simile or metaphor that admirably convey the perceived generalisation is as highly evolved in the Native as in any other human variety.[17]

I think that the magistrates, native commissioners, police officers, missionaries, farmers, miners, and traders in South Africa who have had first-hand experience of dealing with raw Natives will agree with me that in sound reasoning ability, as applied to matters with which he is familiar, the Native is no whit below the white man. It would be easy for me to give hundreds of instances that have come under my own observation of arguments stated and deductions made by Natives who were innocent of all European education that would show a capacity for mental analysis and clear ratiocination equal to that of the educated European, but I have to consider the reader's patience and will therefore confine myself to a few illustrations taken at random from a number that were written down by me at the time of observation. I may say here that my translation

---
[17] "730 Sechuana Proverbs" by Solomon T. Plaatje.

into English has been made with the most scrupulous regard to exactness so as to avoid the possibility of importing into the words used a fuller meaning than that which was actually present in the speaker's own mind.

In the Northern part of Matabeleland, not far from the Zambesi river, lives a tribe called Bashankwe who follow a custom of marriage known locally as " ku garidzela " which is in effect a rendering of personal service, in the doing of such primitive husbandry as there obtains by the prospective son-in-law for the parent of the girl chosen instead of paying for her a consideration in money or cattle as is done by most of the Natives in South Africa. It is a practice similar to the custom which may be supposed to have been general in Palestine when Jacob served for Rachel in the days of the Hebrew patriarchs. Sometime ago I discussed the nature and present incidence of this custom with a chief named Sileya of those parts, a wholly untutored Native. A point brought up for settlement was the validity, under the present *régime*, of the claim for compensation that under their law might be brought by a rejected " garidzela " lover for the value of the work done by him during his period of service when, at the end of such service, he found the girl unwilling to marry him. I had explained to the chief that the white man's government would always set its face against any custom whereby it might be possible for the parents to pledge their daughters in marriage, and had pointed out that this particular custom was for that reason not viewed with favour by the authorities. To this Sileya replied : " If you, the Government, will make it plain that the man who finds himself refused by the girl for whom he has been serving can claim compensation for the work he has done then the fathers will become more careful than they now are and they will refuse to accept the young man's services save where the girl is old enough to consent for herself, for no man likes to give up what he has won and held, and in this manner our old custom will not go against the way of the Government." This reply, which I have Englished almost literally, is typical of the Native form of argumentation and it shows good all-round thinking ability ; it is not a particular instance of special intelligence, but a fair example of average Native perspicacity.

A few months ago, while discussing with some elderly Matabele Natives the subject of miscegenation in South Africa generally one of the old men voiced the opinion of the meeting thus :

" White people do what they like, they take what they like, and when they like certain girls they take them, and what can we say ? And, after all, why should they not do so ? Everything belongs to them, we are their people, our girls belong to them, the white people only take what is theirs to take."

" But," I interpolated, " white men do not take the girls away from you, it is the girls themselves who leave their own kind and go to the white men."

" No," he replied, " I say they take the girls because they know as well as we do that women—all women—will always go where they can live with ease and have plenty and be without work, and this they can do when they go to the white man, whereas with us they must work. Therefore I say that the white men take the girls away from us, but I do not say that they do wrong so long as they only play with them and have no children by them, for it is the manner of all the world that men and women come together and no law can be made to stop them from doing so, but the white men do wrong when they allow the black women to have children by them because such children grow up without proper homes, and that is very sad and wrong."

I think the average white man, whatever his own opinion may be on this matter, will acknowledge that there is clear thought and strong common-sense in the old man's dictum, and this old man is an ordinary raw Native, without any European education.

My good friend, Mahlabanyane, is a typical Tebele of the old school. In his youth he accompanied the hunter Selous on many wanderings, and he never tires of telling of the ways and habits of the game and wild animals he has seen and shot. One day he told me that he had observed all the wild animals of Rhodesia, big and small, and that he had examined them all after they had been killed. He had come to the conclusion, he said, that many of the bigger animals were related to one another in some wonderful way, and that they had probably come out of the earth, all alike, and had then afterwards become different, " as people do when they separate and live always by themselves away from other people," he added.

" Look at the elephant, the rhinoceros, the hippopotamus and the wild pig," he said, " they must at one time have been one kind ; their teeth are alike, and none of them chew the cud. I think they must be cousins to one another, and, one time, perhaps, they were brothers."

Leaving aside the question of the absolute correctness of the old man's observation there can be no doubt that we have here a thinker who, being struck with the physiological similarity of some animals is attempting to account for the fact, and does so along the lines of Darwin and his predecessors, but without any of the facts and theories that were recorded before they began their labours. I asked the old fellow if he had ever heard Selous talk about this matter, and he said he had not ; the idea, he said, had come out of his own head.

One day a Zambesi woman whose husband, a petty chief, was awaiting trial for murder at my station, sent word to me asking for permission to dance that night in the compound. Surmising that there was a religious motive behind this request I gave my consent, and afterwards watched the dancing for an hour or so.

The element of rhythm in sound and movement has always been one of the chief means of exciting and expressing religious exaltation as well as sexual passion, and the two emotions merge easily in all primitive people whether they be the half-civilised moujiks of Russia, or the frequenters of modern "Revival Meetings," or the naked Batonka on the banks of the Zambesi. The Batonka, indeed, are particularly fond of dancing to the beat of the ubiquitous drum.

The woman, who was accompanied by a few of her female friends, danced with unusual grace, and her movements were remarkably free from erotic incitation. Holding a pair of gourds in which little stones rattled not unmusically, like castanets, she gyrated in the moonlight and pirouetted on her toes with such lightness and elegance that my curiosity was roused, and the next morning I had her brought to my office and asked her to account, if she could, for the marked difference between her way of dancing and that of the rest of her people.

This is what she said: " I was very sad and my whole body was heavy. I felt ill, so I asked that I might be allowed to dance. Dancing always does me good when I feel unwell. I did not learn to dance in the way I do from anyone. I think the Great Spirit gave to me the gift of dancing, the power came down on me when I was a child. I have never seen Europeans or Arabs dancing. I have never seen an Arab dancing woman. I dance my way because the Spirit gave it to me to do so."

I then asked her what it was that made her well. Was it the dancing or the profuse sweating which I had noticed? " The Spirit," she said, " made me well, he gave me to dance, the dancing made we sweat thereby cooling my body, and that made me well, it brought my heart back to its right place."

This clear expression of concatenated thought from a Native woman who had had no missionary tuition or other education of the Western kind shows to my mind sound reasoning capacity no less developed than that met with in Europeans generally.

Turning over my notes I select, at random, a few more instances to illustrate my argument.

A Tebele youth of about twenty years of age, smooth-limbed and good looking, was charged some years ago in the Rhodesian High Court with the crime of abducting two young Native girls for his own immoral purposes. I made a note of the chief part of his speech in his own defence at the time. This is what he said:

" I have the gift of singing and dancing, my father had it, and his father before him. When I sing and dance people forget their sorrows, and when I leave a kraal, singing as I go, the people follow me for the joy of my song, so that sometimes I have to drive them away. Now it is easy to drive away old men and women, but who can drive away two pretty girls like these that have been made to speak against me to-day? When I sang and danced at their kraal their father gave me a goat because I had made his heart white and glad, and his daughters followed me and joined in the play—and I am young! When I become old and can no longer sing and dance the girls will not follow me. Why should I not be merry while I may? I never said a word to these girls, they followed me, I did not call them. But now, if the white men who listen to my words feel doubtful about what I say, then I would ask the judge to allow me to show them here and now how I can dance and sing, and if, after hearing and seeing me do so, they still think I am to blame, then I have no more to say; I shall go to gaol with a broken heart, and silent."

The offer made by this African Apollo, I need not say, was not accepted, and he was found guilty and sentenced to a term of imprisonment with hard labour, but I remember that several of the jurymen expressed their astonishment afterwards at hearing so good a defence so pleasingly expressed by a raw Native youth who had never been to any kind of school.

On one occasion I had some trouble to make a Native complainant understand that the evidence upon which he relied was entirely hearsay and therefore of no avail against the man he wished to charge with a crime of theft. While talking an elderly Tebele arrived and I put the matter to him. He listened gravely and when I had finished he turned to the other and said:

"Have you not heard before that that which is heard only cannot be heard again in Court? You must bring witnesses who saw and heard themselves what you say has happened. The words of the man who says he heard the story from another is no testimony against a man when he is to be tried for a crime or a debt."

After writing down this crisp and explicit statement from a Native whom I knew to have had little or no intercourse with educated Europeans I asked the old man if he had ever heard the matter discussed in a European Court. He said he had not, and seemed surprised that I should consider his words worth putting down in a note-book.

When it is realised how few laymen amongst ourselves are able to grasp the distinction between admissible and inadmissible evidence in a Court of Law, and how few would be able to express themselves as clearly as did this old, so-called, heathen, then the instance is seen to be worth citing.

I remember a Native witchdoctor who in defending himself against a charge of alleged witchcraft practice spoke thus :

"The people you have heard to-day came to me and told me that they had had sickness and death at their kraal. I knew these people and I knew that there had been strife among them for a long time over the dividing of an inheritance. I threw the bones[18]—it is our way—and I told these people that the spirit of the old woman, who was the grandmother of most of them, was angry because of the quarrelling that did not cease ; I told them that the snakes, that is to say the ancestral spirits of these people, were angry at the noise of the quarrelling, and I told them to redeem their fault by killing a goat,—it is our way. And now it is said that I have done wrong. In what way have I done wrong ? I have heard a white missionary say that the white man's God sends sickness to people when they sin, and that if the sinners leave off their evil ways then they become well and happy again, and I said the same to these people—and if

---

[18] "Throwing the Bones" is the usual form of divination practised by the Natives in Rhodesia.

they paid me ten shillings, why, do not the whites make payments to their priests?"

I might add, in parenthesis, that the argument advanced did not find favour with the magistrate on the bench who, like so many of his kind, had little knowledge of Bantu lore and languages, and who therefore could only perceive the letter of the law and not the human spirit behind the acts that constituted a breach of the white man's statute.

The Natives, like most of the white people, prefer not to think overmuch about death and whether there be life for us beyond the grave; like the vast majority of Europeans they prefer to take the superstitions and beliefs of their forefathers for granted. Vague notions about ancestral and familiar spirits that emanate from the grave in the guise of snakes or other animals are accepted in the same spirit or traditional mood in which the doctrines and dogmas of the various religions of Europe are accepted by the bulk of white believers.

I have found among the Bantu the same child-like faith in all that is proclaimed by traditional authority about things supernatural, and I have found also among them the

F

same hesitation or inability to believe without questioning in all that is laid down in the name of tradition that we see among ourselves. The will to believe is temperamental and general, but the unbeliever is found among the Bantu as well as everywhere else.

I remember that I asked a raw Native once what he thought about the after-life in which so many white and black people professed to believe. He answered : " The white people are a clever race ; they see many things in their books ; perhaps they can see even beyond death. I do not say that they are liars, as some of our people sometimes say. They may know these things, I do not. All I know is that when I die this breath that is now in me so that I am able to think and speak will leave my body which then must be put away in the ground : I think that will be the end of me—but, not quite, for there," —here he pointed to his infant son who was toddling about in the strong sunlight—" there in him, my son," and his voice grew tender as he spoke, " I shall live on because he is part of me, my life is in him ; I cannot die altogether so long as he lives, but if he should die and not leave a son to carry on my life, then should I die the death utterly."

I recollect that when I wrote these clear words of an honest doubter there came to mind the old Arab saying: "Whosoever leaveth no male hath no memory," which is but a confession of that sense of doubt that has haunted the minds of men of all races and at all times while the people as a whole have professed their hope and belief in a life everlasting.

I discussed the matter of polygamy with a Native youth one day, and made a note of his argument. He said:

"In our district the young women are beginning to go against the man who wants more than one wife. I have a young wife, and when I talk to her about taking a second wife she says that she will not suffer it. She says that the white people do well in that the man and his wife grow old together, whereas we Natives, as she says, we are like the cattle in the kraal; we do not behave like human beings. But to this I answered that our fathers and mothers taught us that one wife by herself cannot be happy and comfortable because when she falls sick, as women often do, there is no one to help her, whereas when a man has two or more wives they can help and nurse one another, they need not be sad or unhappy. I think our fathers way is the good way and I shall follow it, but I know there will be trouble because of the new thoughts my wife has taken from the white people."

Now I do not say that these instances show any remarkable intelligence or power of thinking, but I do say that they show sound level-headed reasoning just like the common sense reasoning from cause and effect which we find in the average European, and that they show, moreover, that the same types of mental disposition and capacity are found in black and white alike.

It would indeed be easy for me to continue giving instances like these to show the essential sameness of the nature of the minds of the black and white people, but I must consider the weight of my book and the readers patience. I have refrained from pointing to those Natives who have proved their scholastic capabilities at various universities and colleges because it is generally surmised that these men are exceptional or that their success is due to a highly developed imitative faculty coupled with a strong memory, with which it is fashionable to credit the successful Native student, and I have advisedly confined myself to instances drawn from the everyday life and thought of the normal and uneducated Native people.

I have lived amongst the Bantu for nearly thirty years and I have studied them closely, and I have come to the conclusion that there is no Native mind distinct from the common human mind. The mind of the Native is the mind of all mankind; it is not separate or different from the mind of the European or the Asiatic any more than the mind of the English is different from that of the Scotch or Irish people. The English way of speaking differs from that of the French, but there is no reason for thinking that the mind of the two people differs in any way whatever. The languages of the world are many but the mind of the world is one.

There are, I know, some white men who talk knowingly about a Native mind which they allege to be unlike their own, a mind of whose strange anfractuosities they profess a special knowledge, but these people must not be taken seriously. They are always half-educated men, suffering, as Cardinal Newman said, from that haziness of intellectual vision which is so common among all those who have not had a really good education. These people pretend to a knowledge which is impossible, seeing that we can only know and understand the minds of other people by assuming that they are like our own so that if we postulate a Native mind different from our own it must of necessity remain unknowable by us, for what is psychology but the power of understanding others from our understanding of ourselves?

The judge on the bench and the priest in the confessional follow the thoughts and feelings of the minds they have to deal with, not by virtue of any special power of divination, but simply by judging their fellowmen's way of thinking and feeling to be even as their own.

The truth of the matter is that all men think in the same way, but not always about the same things. There is no such thing as an inherent racial mind but there are different national and racial cultures lasting sometimes for centuries, like that of China, and some times only for a generation, like that of modern Germany. But these differences are temporary and outward and not inwardly heritable. The difference between the mind of the philosopher and the plough-boy is one not of kind, not even of degree, but of content. The things that occupy the mind of the peasant farmer are not the same that fill the mind of the university don, but if the respective environments of the two types had been reversed the professor might have thought about manure and the farmer about metaphysics. And this holds good also of nations and races. Consider, for instance, the German people who before the rise of Bismarck were looked upon as a nation of peaceful peasants and *Gelerhten,* " *ces bons Allemands,*" in contemporary French parlance, and how they became within a few years through being made to think constantly about their own national supremacy, a race of ruthless warriors that terrorised and nearly conquered Europe in the Great World War. The mind of the German race had not been changed, but the main business of that mind had been changed through the imposition on the growing masses of a new ideal, the ideal of dominion in the hands of the German people.

The difference between the mental status of the white man and the Native is the same as that which we notice between the man who has had a liberal education and the man who has not, and it lies mainly in the fact that the one is given to introspection, analysis and criticism whereas the other, whether he be a European peasant or a Bantu herdsman, looks outward, takes things for granted and asks no questions, so that with the Bantu as with the illiterate European, the primitive thoughts and ways of their forefathers are held good enough by their sons, but this does not preclude the latent potentiality in both for the understanding and acquisition of new thoughts and ways once the shackles of conservatism have been loosened and cast aside.

In his thinking about the things he knows the black man comes to the same conclusion as the white man when he thinks about the same things. The black man does not think about electricity or the differential calculus because he knows nothing about these matters, neither, and for the same reason, does the European peasant wherever he may still be found in his primitive state. It has been alleged in America and in South Africa that Negro and Bantu children, when compared with European children in both countries, show not only comparative slowness in the study of arithmetic, but that they are on the whole less accurate in their work, and this I readily believe, for the reason that the home surroundings of the black children are seldom as favourable to the development of speed and exactness as they are among Europeans. It is not considered "good form" among Natives to do things in a hurry, slowness is regarded as essential to good manners; moreover the craving for speed and exactitude is everywhere a feature of high-pressure city life rather than of life in the country. The town artisan of to-day must be quick and accurate, whereas the agricultural labourer is found satisfactory so long as he is a steady worker, and the home atmosphere of the two types is bound to be affected by these considerations. The home atmosphere of the ordinary Bantu family in process of acquiring the ways of Western civilisation will be more like that of the agricultural labourer than of the town artisan or shopkeeper, and it is conceded on every hand that the home influence has a direct and important bearing on the children's progress in school. Take as an example the children of the back-veld Dutch in South Africa. I have been told by many of their teachers that the difficulty in teaching these children is not so much to make them work as to rouse them to a sense of the importance of speed and accuracy, and yet we often see children from this class growing into men and women of very high intellectual ability.

There are also some who think that the Native has no great capacity for mechanics and engineering generally, but I have seen so many instances of mechanical resourcefulness and inventiveness in Natives who have only had a superficial acquaintance with machinery that I cannot doubt that with technical education like that given to European apprentices they will attain to proficiency equal to that of the whites.

I do not profess the knowledge of a pedagogue in these matters. I speak simply from an insight gained through many years of observation and study at first hand. I have listened to thousands of old Native men of many different tribes in my time, I have heard them speak their inmost thoughts, not through interpreters—who ever learned anything through an interpreter?—I have studied these people in and out of Court, officially and privately, in their kraals and in the veld during many years, and I say that I can find nothing whatever throughout the whole gamut of the Native's conscious life and soul to differentiate him from other human beings in other parts of the world. In his sense of sorrow and of humour, in his moral intuitions, in his percipience of proportion and in all the subtle elements that go to make up the mental constitution of modern man, I see no difference in him from the European variety which to-day stands at the highest point of human achievement, but I freely confess that the African Native has so far shown a lack of that will to think analytically and critically which in the civilised man is the result of a continuous discontent with things as they are, a discontent which has urged him up to his present plane of racial supremacy.

But the reason for the fact that the African Natives have never thought as hard and as long as the ancient and modern peoples of other lands lies not, I think, in a lack of inherent capacity but in a lack of opportunity, the meaning of which now comes to be considered.

Achievement.

We have now come to the point where an answer must be given to the question: If the African Natives are on the whole endowed with a mental capacity equal to that possessed by the Europeans why have they never achieved any civilisation at all comparable with those cultures which have been successively set up by the people of Europe, Asia and Ancient America?

If we take it for granted that the Africans have never achieved a civilisation similar to those that date back beyond the limits of history, a premiss by no means assured seeing that there are signs of cycles of civilisations coming before those of which we have written or monumental records and of whose ethnic origin there is no certain knowledge, then the question may appear to have no other answer than the assumed lack of inherent capacity in the black race, but let us consider the matter closely.

The question asked depends upon the proposition that achievement is the sole test of capacity or, in other words, that achievement must necessarily follow capacity, and this is a proposition by no means free from doubt. It is plain that a desire to achieve is a condition precedent to achievement but it is equally plain that there may well be ability without ambition. The question why civilisation has not followed apparent capacity may with equal propriety be asked about races whose mental abilities have never been doubted. Consider, for instance, two such widely separated races as the Red Indians of our own times and the Northmen who roamed over the seas in the days of Alfred the Great.

The North American Indians, though they achieved no civilisation to be compared with the cultures of Mexico and Peru, yet conserved a very high degree of initiative in other directions. According to competent observers, these people have shown a capacity for wiliness and a power of divination of the obscured workings of nature and of the human mind which have never been surpassed elsewhere. That the high moral and mental status of these people is fully recognised by their European successors is proved by the fact that many Americans in high stations to-day actually boast of having in their veins the blood of the North American Indian. And yet these highly gifted people had not when Columbus discovered America attained to the knowledge of iron. Despite the advantages of a most favourable environment and a stimulating climate, the Red Indians were in point of mechanical development behind the earliest Bantu; they had no iron implements, no tillage and no settled or permanent abodes, and whatever may have been the cause of their lack of development, the fact remains that there was no achievement despite undeniable capacity.

The early Scandinavians who lived in a state of barbarism ages before and long after Egypt, Mesopotamia, India, Greece and Rome developed their various civilisations, furnish another illustration of the fact that there may well be capacity without accomplishment, for no one can doubt the keenness of the minds of these people who have advanced to the front ranks of human endeavour. These rude sea-rovers must have lived in what is generally supposed to have been a most stimulating climate during long ages while other races in Southern Europe and in Asia built up mighty civilisations within environments that seem to have been far less incitative of progress.

Although the broad facts of history are known to us the causes that have contributed in the past to keep down some races while other peoples who were no better endowed or situated rose to the greatest heights of human effort cannot be stated with certainty. It is easy to cite the circumstances that are commonly conjectured as accounting for the origin and growth of civilisation, such as soil, climate and geographical position, but it is equally easy to point to times and places when and where great civilisations have arisen under conditions that have concurred elsewhere with miserable stagnation in rude barbarism.

Climate is, perhaps, the factor which is most generally condescended upon as being the chief of the causes that contribute to that collective accomplishment which we call civilisation, but the connection between the two things is far from clear, indeed it seems to be often negatived by actual facts. Seeing, for instance, that the easy fruition of desire which is possible in tropical and sub-tropical latitudes does away with the idea of necessity as the mother of invention in those parts of the world it becomes difficult to see how tool-using man, who is generally supposed to have originated somewhere in the warm belts, came to take the first and the most difficult steps in the upward progress where there was so little, if any, incentive to that sustained effort and concentration of the mind which is required for the thinking out of the most difficult of all thoughts, the first principles of any art or craft. Why, we may well ask, should the primitive African have worried about cultivating the soil where edible roots and berries abounded? Why should he have bothered about making fire where there was no need of artificial warmth or for the cooking of food? Why should he have cudgeled his brains to fashion weapons and to contrive snares for the killing of game of which he was in no more need than his vegetarian cousins, the anthropoid apes? Why should there have been progress where the environment provided no stimuli therefore, in other words, why should primitive man have moved forward where indulgent nature allowed him to stand still?

If we believe, with Darwin and other students, that our primitive ancestors emerged from somewhere within the warm zones, we cannot avoid the difficulty of reconciling that supposition with the theory that civilisation is in the first instance the result of a stimulating environment. If on the other hand, we surmise that *homo sapiens* originated in the colder parts of the world we still have to account for the fact that his further progress was made not in those parts but in warmer latitudes where a genial climate afforded no apparent provocation for continued effort in the way of invention and general development.

It would seem that the innate tendency to conservatism latent in man, the disposition to leave things as they are and to stick to the familiar devil rather than fly to unknown gods, is in itself sufficient to account for those lapses in mass-achievement and those long periods of stagnation which mark the course of mankind everywhere. We see how Egypt hovered for centuries on the brink of the discovery of the alphabet but never attained thereto. The exponents of the so-called "pulsatory hypothesis" can hardly claim that a change in the climate will explain the fact seeing that the neighbouring people were able to accomplish this great feat under very similar climatic conditions. We see how China developed a wonderful civilisation while the Western world lay steeped in barbarism, and then went to sleep till now. The size of that great country made possible always the friction between people coming from widely separated localities, which we believe to be conducive to progress, and the climate and general environment seems to have been no less favourable than in Europe and America. We see how the Arabs made great conquests and enriched the world with many patient and accurate observations and then came to a standstill and remained as they are to-day in serene contentment, strangers to the very idea of progress. Can it be said that mental capacity and collective will-power were lacking in any of these people? On the contrary, it is admitted that they were possessed of mental powers as great as those of the restless Europeans of to-day who are rushing onward in a ceaseless pursuit of change, a pursuit made possible only by continuous victory over the forces of conservatism, and this victory, as I think, is gained not through the outward circumstances of climate and geographical surroundings, but through a "divine discontent" which is kindled, we know not how, in the leaders of the world, regardless of time and place, as says the poet of one whom he hails as the deliverer of his country:

> "A flaming coal
> Lit at the stars and sent
> To burn the sin of patience from her soul,
> The scandal of content."

It is this inward fire rather than any outward pressure that prompts the captive spirit to break loose from the fetters of the unmoving giant, custom, the greatest of all tyrants, who grows stronger as he grows older. The difficulty of reversing the ways and conditions that have been induced from birth is tremendous, and progress has never been possible without breaking away, always at great risk to the innovators, the stoned prophets of all ages, from the powerful grip of hoary and hallowed custom, which is the essence of conservatism. Initiative implies the breaking of the commandment which enjoins everyone to honour his father and mother that he may live long in the land, a sanction which entails continued adherence to the ancestral ways and ideas, and which, being rooted in instinctive fear of innovation, has power over us all.

Progress, then, has everywhere been the result, in the beginning, of individual initiative in men who were possessed of the power of personality, the " born " leaders of the world who, whether they figured as chiefs or kings, witchdoctors or priests, prophets or lawgivers, were all reformers in their various ways. We see how these restless spirits have appeared everywhere at irregular intervals, not only in localities favoured by nature, but often in the most unlikely places, and there is no reason for thinking that this sporadic cropping up of new leaders will ever cease.

But although we believe that progress has been started always and everywhere by the efforts of reformers that have occurred as spontaneous variations from the dead level of their fellows independent of time and circumstances, we need not deny the effect of environment, especially the effect of an inimical environment, upon a new movement after it has been started, and it may well be that the physical disadvantages of the great "dark" continent may have made difficult, if not impossible, in the past that meeting and friction of different cultures which seem to be essential to the birth of intellectual life, so that here the admitted isolation of the inhabitants during many centuries may have served to squelch initiative and foster stagnation. Nevertheless the influence of environment must not be overrated for we see that general contentment with resulting inertia have existed for untold ages in places where now the sounds and shocks of daily progress reverberate in a thousand fields of civilised activity without any change being discernible either in the bodily or mental calibre of the people themselves, and this must surely teach us that it is not incapacity nor yet unfavourable physical environment, but that, more than anything else, it is the dead weight of human conservatism that holds down a nation or a race to its particular level ; that it is the human element in the general milieu that determines human development, a lesson that has been well summed up in the Chinese aphorism " A man is more like the age he lives in than he is like his father and mother."

Some years ago a theory was advanced which assumed the presence from the beginning of an inherently superior race of blond Europeans who, it was supposed, left their lairs in the North from time to time to harass and conquer essentially inferior people in the South whom they innervated through intermarriage with their superior mentality, and thereby succeeded in rearing those mighty civilisations that waned and fell when the " blue " blood of the invaders became absorbed and lost in the old autochthonous streams. Apart from the lack of cogent evidence this theory, it if may be so called, is unsatisfactory in that it does not explain why these putative super-men failed to establish within their own stimulating environment any of those great cultures that were set up in places and under climatic conditions which are supposed to have been far less provocative to progress. To-day the theories of Gobineau and Houston Chamberlain who both held up the Teutons as being at all times the greatest and noblest of human kind, do not impress the non-Teuton part of the world, nor do the later apostles of the more recent " Nordic " race faith, like Madison Grant, and others of his school, succeed in persuading thinking men and women that the Scandinavians and the English are the only people that ever could initiate and sustain great civilisations. The fact that great civilisations have been built up and are now being developed by people who were and are neither blond nor Nordic makes it impossible to believe these pretensions to exclusive racial genius and merit. " All the talk," says Professor Flinders Petrie, " about Nordic supremacy is vanity when we look at the facts in Europe. Dark Iberians and Picts, Asiatics, Gaels and Celts, are the basis of our peoples. Further, it is in the time of stress and difficulty that the older stocks come again to the top. The majority of the men of power among the Allies have not been fair Nordics but dark men of the underlying races."[19]

Recent study has indeed dissipated that fascinating idyl about the old race of tall, blond Aryans as the originators of our present civilisation, for it has been shown that the so-called Aryan civilisation was inferior in many ways to the primitive culture of neolithic times, and it can now hardly be doubted that our classical civilisation is of Mediterranean origin though Aryanised in speech. It is now generally accepted that history points not to Scandinavia and Germany, but to the lands lying round the Mediterranean Sea as furnishing the matrix out of which civilisation has sprung. It is to the South rather than to the North, to the early people of Egypt, Palestine, Greece and Rome, and not to the primitive inhabitants of Scandinavia and Germany, that we must look for those great men whose intellect and character were strong enough to overcome the natural conservatism of their times. The

---

[19] "What is Civilisation." Article by Professor W. M. Flinders Petrie, in the *Contemporary Review* for January, 1921.

mind of the early white men of the North never soared higher than a valhalla peopled with puerile deities and blood-stained warriors whereas the swarthy thinkers of the South discovered the unseen God, invented art and philosophy and developed law and government. And though the Church proclaims the highest of all born leaders, Christ himself, to be the very son of God, yet was he a native of Palestine and not a fair-haired, blue-eyed Teuton as represented by mediæval painters of Germany and Holland.

It is no doubt true that the invaders and the immigrants have often achieved more in their new surroundings than in their homelands, as the Moors in Spain and the Irish in America, but it must not be forgotten that the civilisation which the new-comers have enriched by virtue of their new found freedom from home conservatism has not been of their making; they may have added thereto but they did not beget it; the spadework, which is the hardest part, had been done before they arrived.

Looking round the world to-day we see clearly that race is not the determining factor in contemporary progress. In Japan we see a people, admittedly not white, who until yesterday were stagnating under a system of childish feudalism, now developing at a great pace a culture similar with and not inferior to that of modern Europe, while in Western Ireland we see white people living in a state of sloth and squalor below that of many " raw " Bantu tribes in South Africa. These facts show that any race, white black, or yellow, may be kept down simply by the forces of conservatism, chief among which is priestcraft operating through prejudice and superstition in the name of religion. To say this is not to cavil at the priests of any particular time or creed. We must have priests as well as prophets. The prophet of a new faith begins his mission by breaking the images of the priests before him and is succeeded by his own priests who set up new images and dogmas wherewith to conserve the new-found creed until it in turn becomes too old when, in the never-ceasing course of evolution, the law of variation bids a new prophet arise. The priest must needs be to preserve the world from the anarchy of too many reformers, but his power, if long continued, tends to inhibit the divine spirit of discontent which makes for human advancement. It is the priest's duty to preserve the old and to hinder the new, and when he finds he can no longer ignore the new inventions that are made around him he will at most accept the new learning as a means only to preserve the old order whose servant he is. The founder of the Society of Jesus enjoined his followers: "Let us all think in the same way, let us all speak in the same manner, if possible," and it is reported of him that he said that were he to live five hundred years he would always repeat "no novelties" in theology, in philosophy or logic, not even in grammar." In Africa priestcraft, in its primitive form of witchcraft, has continued for unnumbered ages to perpetuate the elementary creed of ancestor worship whose chief article is that the ways of the fathers must remain the ways of the children, and that to depart from the old and established order is sinful and wicked, and under this baneful authority progress has been impossible.

But although the heavy conservatism enforced by this primitive cult has smothered initiative during many centuries it does not follow that the mind and character of the African people have been impaired thereby beyond the life of each generation. The mental sloth in which the Western world lay steeped during the dark ages before the Reformation did not become a heritable defect. But apart from the question of the possibility of the transmission of acquired characters we have the fact that within the scope of his daily life the conservative and uncivilised African has to face and solve as many difficult problems as the civilised European in his different surroundings. That these problems are made up of elements differing from those that constitute the problems of the civilised man in his daily avocation proves only a difference of content, not of difficulty. The mental strain involved in leading the so-called simple life of the so-called savage is, on the whole, no less intense than that suffered by the civilised man in maintaining his civilised existence. In the all-surrounding air of superstition and mutual suspicion in which the African moves and has his being he requires cunning to circumvent the cunning of his fellows,—and very deep cunning it sometimes is,—so deep, indeed, that the intellectual European has difficulty in following the dark and devious ways thereof. Vigilance and resourcefulness, careful observation, prudence, forethought, caution, judicious apprizement of character and intelligent calculation of probabilities are required for the planning of the primitive African's daily campaign against the forces of darkness with which he is surrounded, and to carry out these plans he must have courage, firmness of will and self-control in no less measure than the average European city-dweller. To avoid the ever-present chance of being found guilty of witchcraft, which in the past meant always death, the African has had to develop the faculty of lying to a high point of efficiency, and no one who knows him will contend that he is inferior to the European in this respect. The natural education of the Natives include the art of lying as the education of Spartan boys included the practice of larceny. Lying, we know, develops the memory, for a good memory is essential to successful lying. Some of the ruses and stratagems thought out by Natives fleeing from the king's wrath or the witch doctor's doom, of which I have heard from the Natives themselves, have seemed to me to be in subtilty of design and in daring of execution as admirable as any that may be found in contemporary detective fiction, while the fortitude with which defeat and death has been accepted by some of the unfortunate fugitives would evoke admiration in the least impressionable of men. I say therefore that those who deny to the Africans the capacity for sustained collective and purposive effort of mind and body because these qualities have so far not been shown by them in the building up of a civilisation of their own must consider the fact that the nations which to-day lead the world in all the ways of civilisation remained for thousands of years without leaders and without achievement while the people who now lag behind produced those mighty men that led and paved the way to the great civilisations of the past, and I think that we must recognise in that fact a lesson to teach us that present inferiority is no proof of permanent inability, wherefore it may well be that the Natives of Africa will some day rise and compete with their present overlords in the mastery of all the arts and crafts of a modern state.

"But," says the white South African, voicing the general opinion, "this is all very well; the Native may have the brains, but he does not, even now when he has the chance of proving himself, show the same capacity for strenuous and continued effort that the white man has shown. He cannot stand alone; if left to himself he will sink back rapidly into savagery."

That the South African Natives are still in a stage where they cannot stand alone, so that if left entirely to their own devices they would lapse back into barbarism, is not, I agree, open to doubt. But would not the same fate overtake any nation or community, regardless of race, if it were completely cut off from all outside help and influence. The civilised Romans who conquered Britain in the early Christian era, no doubt, looked upon the primitive Britons as a feeble folk when compared with themselves, but the erstwhile slaves have since demostrated their capacity for developing a civilisation utterly beyond the imagination of their foreign masters. Rome was not built in a day.

The rearing of Western civilisation required many centuries, and it can hardly be doubted that if the early builders of the great cultures had been left in isolation instead of being stimulated continually from without through foreign learning and influence neither Ancient Rome nor Modern Europe would have come into being. Isolation has always and everywhere been followed by stagnation and regression and there is no reason for expecting the Natives of South Africa to furnish an exception to the universal rule.

That the average Native is lazy no one who knows him will deny. He is certainly no less lazy than the average European workman who must be compelled by economic pressure to do hard labour. The rough and menial work of the world has always been done through some sort of compulsion, either slavery or some kind of economic coaction, for it is not in human nature, white or black, to work hard at uncongenial tasks unless superior force in some shape or other supplies the driving power. The manual workers of Europe are forced by the economic conditions under which they live to do the heavy and rough work that has to be done—there are very few, even among white men, who like rough work for its own sake—and when we consider how small are the wants of the average South African Native we are often surprised that he works as hard as he does The common expression "As lazy as a kaffir" is counterbalanced by the equally common saying used about a white man who works hard at anything "He works like a nigger," which suggests that there is not much difference between the two races in this respect.

Nevertheless the mental attitude of the average Native undoubtedly enables him to enjoy laziness more than the average European whose early habits have been formed by different influences. Primitive man is a lazy man whatever race he may belong to, and civilisation, which has often been helped on by direct slavery, is indeed itself a system of slavery, under which the toilers are driven to their tasks by the goad of necessity. The fact that many Native youths frequently leave their studies before completing the prescribed course, with the entry "Left school tired" against their names, is often cited as showing that the capacity of the Native for sustained mental effort is not as great as that of the average European, but here, again, it must be remembered that the general conditions and home influences under which the bulk of European boys grow up tend to keep them at their studies whereas the Native school boy is not fortified by similar support. The dread of becoming an "unemployable" through lack of education, which is a forcible spur to effort in both parents and children among the whites, is not felt by the Natives who can always find work to do at wages that will satisfy their ordinary wants, and, moreover, the Native's chance of gaining profit and preferment through being well educated are still few in South Africa, so that where there is neither penalty for failure nor reward for success we cannot expect more effort than we find. When education becomes as general in South Africa as it is among the people of Europe then it will be possible to institute fair comparisons. Education is the discoverer of ability and without the opportunity it gives genius will languish and die unknown, as said that acute observer of human nature, Machiavelli, in speaking about the leaders of antiquity, " Without opportunity their powers of mind would have been extinguished and without those powers the opportunity would have come in vain."[20]

Assuming that the capacity for acquiring Western education and civilisation is no greater in the American Negroes than in the Bantu we may note the opinion of a recent student of the race question in America, as being in point here. In his book " Children of the Slaves," Mr. Stephen Graham says " The fact is, Negrodom has to a great extent qualified to vote. Half the population is sunk in economic bondage and illiteracy, but the other half has more than average capacity for citizenship."[21]

The opinion so often expressed in South Africa that "Education is a kind of thing that doesn't agree with the Nigger" is born of the same feeling that animated the power-holding minorities against the illiterate majorities in Europe not many years ago, and, in justice to the minorities, it must be conceded that the effect of education upon the masses has always been disturbing and often disastrous.

---

[20] " The Prince " by Niccolo Machiavelli.
[21] " Children of the Slaves " by Stephen Graham.

Speaking now from my own experience I can say that I have found no ill-effects from education in Natives ; on the contrary, I have found, as a rule, that the Native who has had an ordinary school education is generally more amenable to precept and admonition than the raw kaffir though less bovinely submissive and therefore more resentful of indignities offered to him. The fact that the educated kaffir comes more often in the way of committing theft and dishonesty than his illiterate brother is in itself sufficient to account for the not unduly large number of theftuous crimes with which he is credited as a class, but on the other hand, the propensity in the primitive male that leads to sexual assaults upon women is undoubtedly checked and lessened by education and school-discipline. Education will bring out and give scope to all that is good and all that is bad in the Native as it has done with the white man. If the Natives have not sunk to those depths of infamy which are disclosed daily in the criminal courts of Europe and America it is not because of want of the usual percentage of criminally disposed people among them but because of want of education and opportunity. Commercial immorality and developed swindling are impossible without a commerce, but the cupidity that begets these forms of vice is not lacking amongst the Natives and waits only for the opportunities which developed commerce affords. The potential capacity for criminality and immorality is indeed no less among the Natives than among Europeans. Theft, arson, murder and rape are the most common forms of crime committed by the Natives to-day because the opportunities for perpetrating systematic fraud are as yet few among them. Unnatural immorality is common enough in the kraals and in the "compounds," for the Natives have their "perverts" as well as the whites. At the Native "beer-drinks" crapulous lewdness is as common as it is in the bucolic orgies of European peasantry. There is no "Native" innocence nor is there any "Native" vice, the virtue and the vice, the capacity and the character of the Native are the human qualities and failings that are common to mankind.

The Native is no more able to withstand the enervating effects of isolation than the

European, he is no more anxious to work hard for small wages, no more and no less capable of honesty and thrift, no more and no less endowed with human virtue, no more and no less cursed with the vices of the world, no more human and no less divine than is his master, the white man.

When Machiavelli asserts in general of men that "they are ungrateful, fickle, false, cowards, covetous, and as long as you succeed they are yours entirely; they will offer you their blood, property, life and children—when the need is far distant; but when it approaches they turn against you." He thought, no doubt, of white men only, but to me his appreciation of the baser side of human nature seems no less applicable to the black people of South Africa, and when, on the other hand, Shakespeare declaims:

> "What a piece of work is man! How noble in reason! How infinite in faculty!"

he also, we may be sure, thought of his own kind, but to me, again, the beautiful words, which usage cannot cheapen, express the wonder I have often felt at the wealth of imagery, the mental grasp, the wisdom and the natural dignity in very many untutored natives I have met with, and it is this experience which makes me believe that the present difference between the Europeans and the Native race is one of degree and not of kind, and that, in the fullness of time, achievement will follow the latent genius with which, as I hold, nature has endowed, in equal degree with ourselves, the great Bantu branch of the human family.

Yet I am no encomiast of the Natives, for I know them to be no better than other people, but search as I may, I cannot find that Native character which is alleged to be inherently different from the white man's character. Did not Mark Twain find, as the most conspicuous result of his travels, that "there is a good deal of human nature everywhere," and is it not true that human nature is everywhere the same?

We are far too apt to exaggerate both in our disparagement and in our praise of backward people. Many people still think, if they think at all, of the South

African Native as a being of the kind imagined by Hobbes when he wrote : " Man in his natural state is towards man as a wolf," and, on the other hand, there are still many who regard him, after the fancy of Rousseau, as a sort of primitive man-child existing in a state of natural innocence from which he is being driven by the corrupting influence of the civilised invaders. But all this is wrong. The Native is not a savage. Even before the whites came to South Africa the Bantu lived in social order under a political system in which the principles of constitutionalism were clearly recognised. To-day the Bantu are simply a race of barbarians in various stages of transition from a crude civilisation to a highly developed civilisation, and we shall do well to remember that the process of transition which we are now witnessing is one in which individual mistakes and failures will be more conspicuous, though no more significant, than the general advance.

Miscegenation.

If it is true that the human nature of the Bantu is no whit different from the human nature of the Europeans then it is a fair question to ask why the two races should not be able to live together in liberty, equality and fraternity as people of one nation or body politic. It is because human nature is governed by laws which, unlike the laws of mathematics, cannot be laid down with certainty that we find ourselves unable to give a positive answer to this question. The human nature of the whites, like the human nature of all races that have been predominant before, is swayed by the feelings of pride and prejudice that arise through differences of complexion, physical appearance and bodily odour, as well as the difference in racial achievement, and these essentially human feelings, if they remain as strong as they now are in South Africa, will render impossible the fraternity that implies the liberty to intermarry, so that there arises for our consideration a second question, namely, whether without full fraternity and social equality the two races may yet live together in the land in political liberty and equality.

We observe from the earliest times a rhythmic play, as it were, of opposite forces that tends, alternately, to build up and to break down and mingle human races, but of the laws that underlie and govern these forces we know little or nothing. On the one hand we see how man has always and everywhere shown what the advocates of so-called racial purity have called "a perverse predisposition to mismate" which has made it exceedingly difficult to classify existing human varieties. On the other hand we see throughout nature how a pronounced disparity between varieties of the same species engenders an aversion from one another of the different varieties which seems to arise, in men and animals alike, through the instinct of sexual jealousy which is probably bound up with the primary instinct of self-preservation. Those people who profess belief in the inherent superiority of a particular race naturally look upon the tendency towards race-blending as a perverse proclivity, while those who think that all men are potentially equal regard it as a wholesome instinct provided by nature to counteract the feebleness and infertility which cause the dying-out of the race that becomes too pure.

Racial antipathy seems to depend in the degree of its strength upon the degree of physical disparity between given races. In the so-called Latin races of to-day, prejudice against black people is certainly weaker than in the blond races of Northern Europe. Is this aversion a matter of absolute instinct or is it an acquired social characteristic and as such liable to change? I think the answer must be that this racial repugnance is not naturally inherent in children, nor in women towards the men of a different kind, nor in men towards the women of another race, but that it arises naturally and spontaneously and, in this sense, instinctively, through the feeling of jealousy which is caused, in both men and women, by fear of losing their natural mates to rivals of both sexes from another and disparate race.

White children who grow up together with Native children certainly have no instinctive feeling against their black playfellows; they have to be taught to look down upon and keep away from the companions of their childhood, a fact which no candid observer will deny. It is also a truism of history that the fair-skinned women of a conquered country, as a rule, will yield themselves easily to the swarthy barbarians who have killed or overcome their husbands and brothers. The many women who in British seaports, and in the German towns that were recently occupied by French coloured troops, have lived and cohabited with African men have proved by so doing that they have had no instinctive racial sense of hostility against black men. It has been stated by independent and competent witnesses, who are corroborated by German newspapers of good standing, that the black troops have a very marked attraction for a large number of German women, and that the German men hate the black men because the German women do not.[22] The fact that white women in South Africa and in the Southern States of America never associate with black men does not, I think, prove that they are controlled by instinctive racial or sexual aversion but rather that women, as a whole, are, by reason of their physical inability to dispute with men the ultimate ratio of all order that lies in brute force, thoroughly amenable

---

[22] *Der Christliche Pilger* of 9th May, 1920, and *Volklinger Nachrichten* of 14th June, 1920.

to the rule of social conventions imposed upon them by their jealous masters. I say this because we see that the aversion that has been inculcated from without tends to disappear wherever the man-established conventions lapse or cease to govern either through the comparatively small numbers of black men being insufficient in certain localities to cause fear in the white men living there, as in some seaport towns, or through the temporary break-down of the customary standards of society brought about by war and revolution, as in those parts of Germany that were recently garrisoned by coloured soldiers.

Nature having cast upon the male the duty of winning and holding the females of his species it is easy to see why the racial feelings of jealousy and ill-will are more positive and more active in the man than in the woman, and this explains, as far as these things can be explained, why white men will allow themselves to cohabit freely with black women to whom they feel naturally attracted but will "see red" and commit murder as soon as they find a black man attempting to gain the favour of a woman of their own colour. " Un adolescent aime toutes les femmes " say the French, and it is generally accepted that man is by nature more inclined to polygamy than woman is towards polyandry, still man and woman are both swayed and motived by the same elemental jealousy that is born of fear of losing something valued; the emotion which Descartes has so well defined as " une espèce de crainte qui se rapport au désir qu'on a de se conserver la possession de quelque bien."

It is, no doubt, true that the thinking white woman, no less than the thinking white man, is led to feel dismay and even resentment against the Natives by apprehension of the possibility of danger to white civilisation through fusion of white and black, but this is a feeling caused by intelligent appreciation rather than by instinctive apprehension, and as such liable to be dispelled by argument tending to show that no real danger threatens. During a recent agitation against miscegenation in Rhodesia a number of letters written by white women appeared in the press from which it was easy to gather that the chief concern of the writers was not the possible degradation of the whites, though this was not overlooked, but rather the simple fact that some white men were cohabiting with black women to the prejudice of the matrimonial chances of eligible women of their own race.

But it is unwise to dogmatise in the realms of social and racial psychology; we have not yet discovered the means for analysing with precision the subtle elements of the human soul. I have used the word instinct here in the sense given to it by William James, who defines it as "the faculty of acting in such a way as to produce certain ends without foresight of the ends, and without previous education in the performance," but when we reflect upon the transitoriness of human instincts, as compared with those of animals, and recognise that the human instincts are, as James also says, implanted in us for the sake of giving rise to habits, and then to fade away, we see how difficult it is to draw a line between the instinctive and the acquired or habitual mood or feeling.

If we believe that racial antipathy is caused by the feeling of jealousy that arises instinctively, so to speak, from man's inner nature, then it is safe to say that it will last as long as the substance from which it springs, and as long as the racial difference which provokes it remains, but this belief is not firmly established in the general mind. The whites, as a whole, feel far from sure about the permanence of their cherished pride and prejudice of race; they are, more or less consciously afraid that the antipathy upon which they rely may become weakened and eventually dissipated by close contact of the two races in places where economic pressure has reduced both to the same level of life. We shall do well to remember the words of Renan when we try to estimate the truth of this matter, "La verité consiste dans les nuances," for both estimates may be true; the racial instinct may have to yield here and there to the superior force of economic pressure, and may yet in the main prove powerful enough to prevent the contact that tends to render it of no effect.

The racial feeling which we are considering is undoubtedly much stronger at present in the whites than in the Bantu, but there is reason to believe that the awakening desire for racial self-assertion which we call pride of race will grow and increase in the Bantu as it has done in the Negroes in the Southern States of America, and elsewhere. General education, so far from hindering the growth of nationalism and racialism seems in some sort to subserve and foster that growth; witness the strident self-assertion of the newly-constituted little nations in Europe, and the cult of "Nationalism" in South Africa to-day. It is natural for birds of feather to flock together and screech together. and in the same way throughout mankind particular groups of people tend naturally to keep together and to marry among themselves separately from the rest of the community by which they happen to be surrounded, and this ethnic instinct, if so it may be called, is seen to operate even where, as among the Italian immigrants in America, there is no great racial difference between them and the Native-born inhabitants, and, much more markedly, in the Southern States of America where, according to a recent observer, the present tendency is not towards but away from miscegenation, so that the ultimate blending of colour is not likely to take place there in the course of nature.[23]

---
[3] "Children of the Slaves" by Stephen Graham.

The normal Native man does not hanker after white women, and the normal Native woman is not, as a rule, anxious to mate with a white man, but this normal disposition is apt to be disturbed by the familiarity which is bred by the close contact that occurs in towns and other centres. It is not, therefore, safe to deny the possibility that with advancing industrialism in congested areas there will be some white women ready to marry or cohabit with Native men who are either in positions of relative superiority or in possession of more money than their white fellow-workers or neighbours, making it possible for them to outbid these in the providing of comparative ease and luxury, which things have always appealed strongly to women of all races. Yet I think that those who prophesy the speedy merging of the two races in South Africa do not give sufficient weight to the fact of the collective consciousness of a racial entity which, being strongly established in the European section, is also being fostered and increased in the Natives by the civilisation which is now spreading among them, so that it seems reasonable to expect that the European aversion from racial blending will be reciprocated from the Native side more and more as time goes on, and that this reciprocal feeling will go far towards keeping the two races biologically intact. I think, therefore, that despite the conditions that conduce to miscegenation, the factor of the growing and reciprocal desire in both races to remain ethnically separate will gain the day.

Many people think that the coloured people in South Africa, who are most numerous in the vicinity of Cape Town, but are also scattered all over the country, will form, as it were, a bridge between the two sections of the population for their eventual coalescence. But when this conclusion is closely examined it is seen to rest on debatable premises, for it is admitted that by far the greater part of the miscegenation that is now going on is between white men and coloured or black women and not between coloured or black men and white women, from which it follows, as has been pointed out by Boas,[24] that, as the numbers of children born does not depend upon the numbers of men but upon the numbers of women, the

---

[24] "The Mind of Primitive Man" by Franz Boas.

result will be a bleaching of the black element, here and there, and not a darkening of the whites in South Africa.

Statistics have, indeed, been quoted which show that between the year 1904 and the year 1911 the coloured population increased in the Cape Province by fifteen per cent. while the total population increased by only six and a half per cent., but these figures do not show how much of the coloured increase is due to propagation among coloured people themselves and how much to unions between white men and coloured women. When it is noted that in the year 1911 the European increase over the year 1904 in the whole Union of South Africa was 14·28 per cent., and that of all non-European elements only 15·12 per cent., it will be seen that although the black increase is on a larger basis it hardly justifies alarm over an imagined flood of overwhelming coloured numbers.

If the coloured increase is due chiefly to propagation among the coloured people themselves then it forms a good argument against those who assert that the half-caste is relatively inclined to sterility, while if the increase is found to be due to cohabitation of white men with coloured women then it is a fair illation that the coloured section is in process of absorption by the whites. This assumed process of absorption will, no doubt, entail the presence of a certain, even a large, number of coloured people for many generations to come, but this number will grow smaller, and not greater, as time goes on because there is no reason to doubt that the white women of South Africa, as a whole, will refrain in the future as they have refrained in the past from cohabiting with black men, so that the observed tendency towards the diffusion of the coloured element back into the parent streams will be allowed to continue.

But let us for a moment look calmly, and as far as possible without prejudice, at the people who in South Africa are said to furnish the awful example of the alleged evil of the crossing of white and black. The fact that the denunciation of these people is based on opposite and contradictory arguments shows that it is not the result of clear thinking. On the one side it is vehemently asserted that the coloured man is a physiological misfit, a sort of hybrid unfit for the society of either white or black, and an alleged relative sterility of his kind is advanced as proof of this assertion. On the other side it is said, with equal vehemence, that the coloured people are mongrels, unfit to mingle with the pure parental breeds, and that this is proved by their excessive fecundity. The coloured people are also accused of being inferior in physical constitution when compared with either of the parent races, and therefore undesirable.

My own observations, corroborated by the opinions of many other observers, leads me to believe that the fecundity of the coloured people is neither greater nor less than that of other people—white, black or yellow—whose birthrate is not artificially restricted, and that their general physical constitution, when not undermined by disease or stunted by underfeeding, is as strong as that of any other human variety. The great naturalist, Wallace, has insisted that some degree of difference favours fertility, but that a little more tends to infertility, and by applying this hypothesis to the facts as I have observed them I am led to believe that there is no biological difference between the Bantu and the European of a degree sufficient to produce any difference, one way or the other, in the fertility of the offspring of the two races, but proper statistics, continued over several generations, will, of course, be required to prove or disprove this conclusion.

The gravest, and, as I think, the most unjust of the many charges brought against these people by an unthinking public, is that the half-caste, wherever he is found, partakes of all the vices but of none of the virtues of his parents. When we remember that in the towns of South Africa the coloured people of necessity form the class that in the nature of things is peculiarly exposed to the temptations of prostitution and crime, then it becomes a matter for wonder that these people are as good and as law-abiding as indeed they are. People who know South Africa will admit that the coloured girl is from childhood exposed to the temptation of loose-living far more than either the Native girl in the kraal or the European girl in her home, and that the coloured boys and youths, by reason of the lack of the right kind of home-influence, which is the result of the unfavourable position in life of the bulk of their parents, naturally gravitate towards the levels where it becomes difficult to avoid crime. But despite all these adverse conditions that press so heavily against them the coloured people of South Africa, taken as a whole, stand justified of the calumnies uttered against them. The coloured people as a whole are not behind the whites in anything except in the lack of opportunity for education and self-improvement, a lack caused not by themselves, but by their inimical surroundings.

That many of the coloured people are immoral and shiftless need not be denied; the same may be said about the "poor whites," who as a class perplex well-meaning legislators, but neither of these proved accusations give reason for thinking that either of these classes is inherently inferior to their more favourably-placed fellow-beings. We must always remember the tremendous handicap of being reared in the depressing surroundings of sloth and squalor. I have seen hundreds of poor whites—as white as any blond German could wish to be—who seemed utterly unfit for the complexities of civilised life, but I have also seen many of the children of these people who, after being removed from their home surroundings, have risen to positions of usefulness and trust, in which they have earned reputations for integrity and capacity. The trenchant saying of a British working-man is in point, "Treat a man like a dog and he will behave like a dog," and the corollary is equally true, that if you treat a man as a man he will, as a rule, rise and quit himself like a man.

The familiar cry that once white blood is diluted with black it is "all up" with our civilisation is not convincing when we remember that the ground-work of this civilisation was built up by races that were not "pure white"; that the white civilisation during the dark ages sank to a very low level through no dilution of African blood, and that it was a mixed race, the Moors, who brought back into Europe the lost principles of Aristotelian science on which the crumbling structure of European culture was rebuilt. To believe that the people of Asia and of Africa may be capable of attaining to Western civilisation, but that the offspring produced by the crossing of these races with whites will not have the necessary capacity therefor is to me impossible. So far from being deterrent to mental growth it would seem that an infusion of African blood in the European serves rather to increase mental capacity; at any rate, those who know South Africa well will not deny that an unmistakable tincture of African blood in a white family is often associated with marked intellectual ability. Against this concession it has indeed been alleged that, while it must be admitted that a small admixture of black blood in a white race enriches it, a small admixture of white blood in a black race degrades it, but this fanciful notion has not been supported by scientific data. The truth of the matter is that as the blacks are the underdogs, the half-breed becomes a racial and social bastard, as indeed he is openly named in South Africa, a man condemned before he is tried, handicapped from birth in a way that would drag down and keep under most of those who shout loudest about their racial superiority. It is his condition and not his nature that keeps the coloured man underneath.

To the man who in face of the facts of history and of to-day believes that all we have of civilisation we owe to the Teutonic or to the Nordic type of man, and that nothing good can ever come out of coloured Nazareths, the possibility of the whites in South Africa becoming browned by the selective agency of tropical light or by an infusion of African blood, no doubt, seems an evil to be prevented at any cost, but those who, like myself, have seen coloured women working in their homes as thriftily and self-sacrificingly as the best of our own women, and coloured men labouring steadily against heavy odds to improve their condition, have become convinced that the coloured people of South Africa suffer under no inherent disabilities when compared with the whites, and for this reason we cannot join in the general wail over a predicted evil which we regard as exaggerated in itself and not, moreover, likely to happen. I would not, however, be taken to advocate the inter-breeding of white and black. Those who have witnessed the misery and suffering which the coloured people have to endure for being coloured will welcome any fair means of preventing miscegenation in South Africa. Proscriptive legislation has been advocated by both the detractors and the defenders of the half-breed, as a means of preventing what both schools, for their different reasons, regard as wrong and undesirable, but I cannot agree that it can ever be right or expedient to penalise and make criminal a natural act which under existing conditions is in many places unavoidable.

There can be no doubt that the evil of miscegenation in South Africa has been greatly exaggerated, both in respect of its nature and its extent, but, nevertheless, so long as the racial prejudice of the white man remains as strong as it is to-day—and there is nothing to show that it is likely to decrease in the future—so long will it be the duty of all good citizens to discourage by persuasion and precept the production of children for whom the ruling race has no love and little pity. Even those among the whites who, in a spirit of good will and tolerance urge that the coloured people should receive preferential treatment because of the white blood which is in them, cannot escape having their point of view warped by their racial prepossession, for, surely, it is not because of a man's class or colour that he is treated as a man to-day but because of his being a civilised member of a civilised community. Nevertheless, the day when civilisation shall be the sole qualification for full membership of the civilised community of South Africa is not yet.

I say, therefore, in answer to the question whether, without the full fraternity which seems impossible here, the white and the black races may not live together in South Africa in political liberty and equality, that the trend of events leads to the belief that the established pride of race of the whites, and the growing pride of race among the Natives will conduce to voluntary separation wherever this is possible, and that in this way the coming generations will contrive to live territorially separate under a common governance, founded upon political equality and liberty.

Conclusion.

The evidence before us leads inevitably to the conclusion that there is nothing in the mental constitution, or in the moral nature of the South African Native, to warrant his relegation to a place of inferiority in the land of his birth, but the same evidence also leads to the conclusion that the racial antipathy which prevails to-day will remain unaffected by this admission, seeing that this racial animosity is caused not by alleged mental disparity but by unalterable physical difference between the two races.

It is important that this distinction be grasped for it goes to the root of the matter. It is the marked physical dissimilarity of the black man that rouses the fear and jealousy of the white man, and not any inherent mental inferiority in him. And we must take human nature as we find it, inscrutable and immutable as it is ; wherefore we must reckon with, and not hastily condemn, the imponderable purpose of a fundamental instinct which is older than speech and deeper than thought, so that, although we admit that this racial antipathy is not justified by logical reasoning, we may nevertheless recognise it as a feeling grounded in man's inner nature—in his heart, so to speak—hardening it against other men whom he feels he cannot receive and entreat as brothers ; in other words, we may say that this feeling is not the result of ratiocination but of forces that are deeper and more elemental than reason ;

that it is a hardening of heart rather than a mental conviction, in which sense we may apply the words of Pascal " Le caeur a ses raisons que la raison ne connait pas."

Now if I am right in thinking that this racial feeling is engendered instinctively by physical dissimilarity only then we may not expect it to be removed or even lessened by the increased and general advancement of the Natives, for although we may hope that the whites will gradually come to recognise the abstract justice of the civilised Natives' claim to full racial equality we must, at the same time, remember that the increasing competition of the black man in every walk of life is bound to bring into play and accentuate the natural race prejudice of the white man whereby the tolerance and good feeling that might otherwise result from a growing recognition of the civilised Natives' mental and moral worth will be more than negatived. The present state of affairs in the Southern States of America is a warning against easy optimism in this respect. We must expect clashing and growing ill-will rather than social serenity to be the outcome of a continued policy of drift.

To condemn the wrong of repression would to-day be like preaching to the converted. Most people now admit that the Africans are entitled, no less than the Europeans, to develop themselves as far and as fully as they can, but the question remains how they can be allowed to do so without intensifying present antipathy on both sides. Parallelism is a word that has been used a great deal of late to signify an attitude of mind, as I take it, rather than a definite policy or plan of action, through which it is hoped that separate scope for civilised activity and development may be given to the Natives on lines parallel to those along which the whites pursue their separate course, but without any forced territorial separation of the two people. Metaphor of this kind is undoubtedly useful to the political speaker in that it enables him to be apt without being exact, and thereby frees him from the possibility of being pinned down to a stated position, but in serious discussion exactness rather than aptness is desired, and to the thinking man the figure of speech, by which the notion of two lines running always parallel without meeting is applied to the course of development of two races living together in one country, is not convincing.

This idea of parallelism is based on the presumption that the ruling race can so rule itself that by the mere exercise of its collective will-power it can refuse always to mix socially with the growing numbers of civilised Natives living and working in the same localities, and thereby—in a manner not yet explained—avoid always the clashing and ill-will that seems inseparable from the close contact of two dissimilar races competing against one another in one country. The advice offered from afar is that the whites should allow the Natives equal opportunities with themselves in all the ways of civilised activity, but—should not invite them home to dinner. Being based on an unwarranted presumption parallelism here begs the question, for it is precisely the ability of the ruling race to follow this counsel of perfection that is in doubt. It is easy to urge that the Europeans must maintain their position in South Africa as " a benevolent aristocracy of ability," but we want to know how this can be done. A recent contributor to the general question of colour has stated that the true conception of the inter-relation of white and black races should be "complete uniformity in ideals, absolute equality in the paths of knowledge and culture, equal opportunity for those who strive, equal admiration for those who achieve; in matters social and racial a separate path, each pursuing his own inherited traditions, preserving his own race-purity and race-pride; equality in things spiritual; agreed divergence in the physical and material."[25] But, again, we want to know how this abstract conception is to be put into actual practice in this world of things as they are.

I have said that the Natives do not hanker after intimate social intimacy with the whites, but this does not mean that the civilised black man who has risen to the economic and educational level of the European remains indifferent whenever his claim to ordinary social recognition is denied or ignored. He would not, indeed, be human if he did not feel hurt whenever he is slighted and treated with contempt by people from whom he differs only in his physical appearance and

---

[25] "The Colour Problem" by Sir F. D. Lugard, in *Edinburgh Review* for April, 1921.

colour. In one of his essays, dealing with Native matters, Professor Jabavu, a Native, describes how "high" feeling arose among the Native teachers and boys in a certain training institution in South Africa at which he had been invited to lecture because he was not allowed to see the inside of the European principal's house, despite the fact that he had ten years of English university life behind him.[26] Such feeling is only natural and must tend always to create ill-will, and, knowing how strong is the convention of the whites against social recognition of the educated Native, we must expect increased bitterness in the future, rather than growing good-will.

The thinking white man, who would fain be just to every one, is perplexed by two conflicting emotions. He feels that the clean-living, law-abiding, educated Native is a man not inferior to himself whom he therefore ought to recognise as a fellow-citizen, but whenever he sees this fellow-citizen aspiring or laying claim to the social recognition that involves contact with white women he is filled instantly with wrath which he can-

---

[26] "The Black Problem" by Professor D. D. G. Jabaou.

not justify to himself and yet cannot suppress. It is easy to see that where instead of common courtesy and mutual recognition from one another of two sections of a community, constant irritation and ill-will result, there the existence of the whole is threatened with disaster. Under such conditions we must expect, not parallel progress, but strife and enmity ; not peace, but a sword.

The Jews may be cited to show how a separate and peculiar people may be able to live together with other races without either clashing with or being assimilated by these but we must remember that the ethnic difference between the Jews and Europeans are too slight to sustain serious and lasting race-antipathy. Parallelism, when applied to the Native problem of South Africa, is clearly nothing more than the old, plan-less drift continued in the pious hope that human nature will sooner or later change into something better than what it is to-day. But human nature will not change. We must never leave passion out of account. If we recognise love we must recognise hate also as a moving force of mankind. Neither must we overlook vanity and arrogance. The white man, being human, will not cease to be vain and ambitious, he will not cease to feel the hatred that comes from the fear of losing possession of his mates, and possession is the natural man's definition of love. Where there is a sense of possession there will also be jealousy and hate, and it will only be by securing the white man in his sense of racial integrity that peace and good-will can be made to last.

Territorial separation of the home-life of the two races is the only way by which parallel development can take place. Some of the Native leaders who have opposed this policy have done so in the belief that their people might eventually be able to prove and enforce their claim to full racial equality, but they have not realised that this claim will be denied always on physical grounds, and not on considerations of moral worth. These leaders mean well but they do not see well. Smarting under the pain of their treatment they do not perceive that the real issue is one of unalterable physical disparity.

The hardships and disabilities under which the educated Native suffers in the Northern Provinces of the Union and in Rhodesia are patent and serious. It is hard that a civilised man may not travel in his own country without a "certificate"; it is hard that he must do only rough or menial, but always ill-paid, work when he is capable of doing skilled and well-paid labour; it is hard that when he is allowed to do skilled labour he cannot claim the wages of a skilled labourer; it is hard to be denied always the privileges of a civilised existence for which he has proved himself fit and worthy; it is hard to be treated always as an inferior and an alien in the land of his fathers; all this is hard, but—'tis the law, written and unwritten, made and enforced by the dominant race, and there is no reason to think it will be made less hard as the pressure of black competition increases.

But if good and ample land can be set aside in the various territories of spacious South Africa in which the Natives can live and move without let or hindrance; in which they can do what work they like for themselves and for their own people; in which they can engage, according to their individual desires, in all kinds of trades and commerce without the prohibition of the white man's colour-bar; in which they can earn the wages that are governed by the laws of supply and demand only ; in which they can build up after their own fashion courts of law and political councils for themselves ; in which, *in fine* they can live and work out their own salvation, unhurried and unworried by strange and impatient masters, then, surely, the Natives of South Africa will have gained a great gain, far greater than any they can ever hope to win by pitting their undeveloped strength against the organised resistance of the whites.

The policy of territorial separation, which is now part of the law of the Union of South Africa,[27] is the only policy that will make

---

[27] When General Smuts introduced his Native Affairs Bill in the Union Parliament in May, 1920, he said, *inter alia*, that he hoped that under a policy of territorial separation, which was now the law of the land, it would be possible to carry out the idea of parallel institutions for the Natives by means of which they could deal with their own concerns. In the course of his speech General Smuts also said " the Pass laws do the Whites no good and are intolerable to the Natives." The Native Affairs Act of 1920 provides for the establishment of a permanent Native Affairs Commission, and for the Creation of local Native Councils or conferences of Native Chiefs and other representatives for the discussion of all questions affecting the interests of the Natives. In explaining the nature and scope of this Act the Prime Minister said that more study and investigation, and more consultation with the Natives were required before it could be said that the areas suggested by the Beaumont Commission were fair and proper.

possible a home existence for the Natives in their own homeland, for we know that, however educated and however worthy the civilised Native may become, he cannot hope to find a home, or to feel at home, among the whites. Rightly or wrongly, the whites have banged, bolted and barred their doors against the blacks, and neither moral worth nor educational qualifications will serve to open them. But in their own areas the Natives will have their own homes and their own home-life, without which human existence is indeed miserable. Those among them who long for the privilege of private ownership will be able to acquire land in freehold in localities set aside therefor, while those who cling to the old ways will be allowed to continue as before under their old system of communal land tenure.

With freedom of movement and action under a minimum of European supervision and control the Natives will, in their own areas, have full opportunity and scope for the development of a home-civilisation of their own along lines similar to, if not identical with, those by which the Europeans follow their separate ways. It is a heroic plan, and it will demand great sacrifice from both peoples, but who can doubt that the end will be worth the effort? The Natives may in some places have to leave the land where their ancestors are buried, and the whites will, in many places, have to accept the price of expropriation for land and houses hallowed and made precious by effort and memories, but the great general gain at the end will undoubtedly be worth all that must be surrendered now. This policy is the only one that holds out hope of peace and happiness for both races. If the fears and objections that are being raised by a few Natives and by individual Europeans here and there are allowed to frustrate this, the only practical plan so far devised, the future generations of both white and black in South Africa will assuredly curse the day their fathers wavered and failed to make the only just and fair provision that could be made.

To those, who for religious reasons feel doubtful about the righteousness of a plan that denies to the Natives the privilege of social equality which is implied in the ideal of the brotherhood of man, I would quote the words of Paul who, when speaking at Athens of the separation of the sons of Adam, said that God " hath made of one blood all nations of men for to dwell on all the face of the earth, and hath determined the times before appointed, and the bounds of their habitations,"[28] for, whether we take this statement to be the inspired utterance of a holy apostle, or simply the reasoned opinion of an acute observer, we must admit that the words convey the experience of the ages that races which are physically dissimilar tend naturally, and therefore, rightly, to dwell apart within their respective racial boundaries.

Some people have professed to be afraid that the territorial separation of the two races will tend to consolidate the Natives, and thereby foster animosity towards the whites which may eventually lead to open war, but this fear seems to have no ground in reason, because it is not proposed, nor, indeed, would it be physically possible, to segregate the Natives by themselves in one great area. On the contrary, it is proposed to dispose of the Natives, as far as

---

[28] Acts 17—26.

possible, according to present geographical and tribal conditions, in several and separate territories, so that race-consolidation of a kind inimical to the whites will naturally be less likely to occur where the Natives live as separate tribes, speaking their different languages, than where, as in the Southern States of America, the Negroes have English as a common medium for the expression of a common race-interest.

Other people, again, are in doubt as to whether the Natives, as a whole, approve of this policy by which their future existence is to be shaped and determined. The answer is contained in the words of Sir William Beaumont, in his report of the findings of the Native Lands Commission, which gathered evidence from all concerned in 1916, where he says "The great mass of the Native population in all parts of the Union are looking to the Act (the Act providing for territorial separation) to relieve them in two particulars—the first is to give them more land for their stock, and the second is to secure to them fixity of tenure."[29]

---

[29] Native Lands Commission. Minute by Sir W. H. Beaumont.

Regarding the Natives of Rhodesia I am able to say that all the elderly Native men with whom I have spoken about this subject— and I have conversed with a large number— agree that the policy, as outlined in the Native Lands Act and the Native Affairs Act of 1920, as I have explained it to them, is good and sound.

It is true that certain prominent Natives of the educated class have protested strongly against this policy, but it is not true that these men have spoken on behalf of the Natives as a whole; indeed, it is safe to say that the vast bulk of the Natives of South Africa have even now no clear knowledge of the legislation that has been made recently in the pursuance of this policy. The protests that have been made from the Native side, moreover, have been directed against the hardship caused through harshness in carrying out the Act in certain places, and against the relative smallness of the areas proposed for Native occupation, and not against the principle itself, and there can be no doubt that the statement quoted from the Report of the Native Lands Commission conveys the true feeling of the large majority of the Natives.

These are some of the objections that have been raised to the policy of territorial separation, but the gravest danger to the successful working of that policy remains to be mentioned. It is the possibility that the cupidity of the whites may lead them to remove their black neighbour's landmarks in the event of the discovery of new fields of gold or other valuable minerals within the Native areas. The danger of such a lapse from the righteousness that exalteth a nation can only be averted by the constant exercise of the public conscience of the whites themselves.

No reasonable person will expect that this policy will do away entirely with all the little troubles that arise from the clashing of opposite racial interests. In the white areas the Native, who can come there only as a labourer or visitor, not as a settler, will remain subordinate to the whites, but his unavoidable competition in trade and industry may nevertheless lead to friction now and then, and the continuance of the present pin-prick policy of enforcing humiliating pass-laws and similar racial restrictions will certainly lead to trouble. But if tolerance and honesty prevail in our councils we shall be able to adjust and settle the many questions that are bound to arise from time to time through the juxtaposition in the industrial field of the two immiscible elements.

But I must come to an end. I have tried to show that there is good reason for accepting the Bantu as the equals of Europeans in every respect save past achievement, but that because of unalterable physical disparity, and not because of any mental inequality, the whites and the blacks cannot live in peace and good-will together in one place, wherefore it follows, as a necessary conclusion, that territorial separation is the only way to lasting peace and happiness in South Africa. I say, therefore, that the black man's place in his own country must be assigned not below, nor above, but apart from that of the white man, for that which nature has made separate man may not join together. I have endeavoured also to show that there is good reason for believing the Bantu to be no less capable of adopting and adapting Western civilisation than other races which in the past have risen from rude barbarism to high culture, but here I admit that the full proof of my belief must be given by the Natives themselves.

The difficulties in the way are many and serious, but if we of the power-holding race remain true to the great principles of justice and fairness which have guided our forefathers in their upward path we shall not go astray. So long as we remember the lesson of history voiced in the saying of the Romans "As many slaves so many enemies" we shall refrain from the means of repression which have always reacted adversely on the repressors ; we shall realise that we cannot set artificial barriers in the way of the civilised Native if he proves that he has the capacity for going higher and the will to try, and we shall learn to treat him, not as a slave, nor as a child, nor yet as a brother in the house, but as a man. The Natives can in fairness demand no more, the whites can in fairness yield no less.